STORIES IN AMERICAN HISTORY

THE
AMAZING
UNDERGROUND
RAILROAD

KEM KNAPP SAWYER

Enslow Publishers, Inc.
40 Industrial Road
Box 398
Berkeley Heights, NJ 07922
USA

http://www.enslow.com

Original edition published as *The Underground Railroad* in 1997.

Library of Congress Cataloging-in-Publication Data

Sawyer, Kem Knapp.
The amazing Underground Railroad / Kem Knapp Sawyer.
    p. cm.
Includes bibliographical references and index.
Summary: "Read about how slaves from the South tried to escape to freedom by use of what became known as The Underground Railroad"—Provided by publisher.
ISBN 978-0-7660-3951-3
1. Underground Railroad—Juvenile literature. I. Title.
E450.S28 2012
973.7'115—dc23   2011020379

Paperback ISBN 978-1-4644-0021-6
ePUB ISBN 978-1-4645-0470-9
PDF ISBN 978-1-4646-0470-6

Printed in United States of America

102011 Lake Book Manufacturing, Inc., Melrose Park, IL

10 9 8 7 6 5 4 3 2 1

Acknowledgments

I would like to thank the many people who helped me with this book— Donna Wells and Joellen Bashir at the Moorland-Springarn Research Center at Howard University in Washington, D.C.; Sally McDonough at Mount Vernon in Virginia; Frances Parker, director of the Sandy Spring Museum in Maryland; Jean Dibble at the United Church on the Green in New Haven, Connecticut; Lynn Nettleton at the Chatham Cultural Centre in Ontario, Canada; Aloysia Hamalainen; and Tony Cohen. And very special thanks to Jon, Kate, Eve, and Ida Sawyer.

To Our Readers: We have done our best to make sure all Internet addresses in this book were active and appropriate when we went to press. However, the author and the publisher have no control over and assume no liability for the material available on those Internet sites or on other Web sites they may link to. Any comments or suggestions can be sent by e-mail to comments@enslow.com or to the address on the back cover.

♻ Enslow Publishers, Inc., is committed to printing our books on recycled paper. The paper in every book contains 10% to 30% post-consumer waste (PCW). The cover board on the outside of each book contains 100% PCW. Our goal is to do our part to help young people and the environment too!

★ CONTENTS ★

A view of the Niagara River from the New York side. Once fugitive slaves set foot in Buffalo, they only had to cross the Niagara River to reach Canada and freedom.

1

THE ESCAPE

The foghorn signaled the impending arrival of the steamboat at the dock in Buffalo, New York. A few minutes later, a loud, grating sound erupted as the crew lowered the plank. The paying passengers gathered their belongings and departed. Little did they know that hidden among them were three fugitives from slavery. Each step the fugitives took along the plank brought them that much closer to their long-sought liberty. Once they set foot in Buffalo, they had only to cross the Niagara River to reach Canada. Although the North offered a measure of freedom to those slaves from the South, Canada promised safety and a new beginning.

The man who had made this opportunity possible was a fugitive named William Wells Brown, who worked as a crew member of a Lake Erie steamboat that ran out of Cleveland, Ohio. "It is well known that a great number of fugitives make their escape to Canada, by way of Cleveland," he later wrote.

And while on the lakes, I always made arrangement to carry them on the boat to Buffalo or Detroit and thus effect their escape to the "promised land." The friends of the slave, knowing that I would transport them without charge, never failed to have a delegation when the boat arrived at Cleveland. I have sometimes had four or five on board at one time.[1]

William Wells Brown recalled that in 1842, between the first of May and the first of December, he ferried sixty-nine fugitives across the lake, assisting them in completing the last leg of their journey. The fugitives he helped rescue often had been on the road for many weeks. In some cases, months had passed since they had last been under a slave owner's command, subject to his every whim, and prisoner to the whip. Most had made

This is an albumen silver print of the "The Underground Railroad," a painting by Charles T. Webber. It depicts fugitive slaves assisted by a group of whites. The reproduction shows two copyright stamps from the Library of Congress, dated 1893.

some part of their long journey by foot—through woods, across unknown territory—and some had traveled by covered wagon or other conveyance. Few, if any, escaped without help of some kind. Aid came from all quarters in the form of food, shelter, and transportation. Some men and women devoted their lives to this cause, while others simply reached out to a person in need.

The system that provided these links between strangers and enabled the slaves to escape was called the "Underground Railroad." Beginning in the first part of the nineteenth century, escaped fugitives, as well as other opponents to slavery, found ways to rescue those held in bondage. Some would sneak back to slave territory and serve as guides to free land; others opened their homes to fugitives who needed shelter. All participated in clandestine operations and expanded the increasingly intricate network of the Underground Railroad.

William Wells Brown's Escape

William Wells Brown was born in the early 1800s in Lexington, Kentucky, the son of Elizabeth, a slave, and George Higgins, a white relative of her master. At his birth his mother gave him the one name of William. Before long their master moved to a large farm in Missouri, taking with him the forty slaves he owned. There William worked as a house servant and his mother as a field hand. Once, when his mother arrived at the

field ten to fifteen minutes late, she received ten lashes with a whip. William was close enough to hear the whip and later wrote, "The cold chills ran over me, and I wept aloud."[2] Later young William was hired out to a Major Freeland in St. Louis, Missouri. Freeland, quick to lose his temper, frequently abused his slaves. One time William ran away into the woods but was chased by bloodhounds and captured. The major flogged him, and then his son "smoked" him—tying him down near a fire of tobacco stems and making him breathe the smoke until he coughed and wheezed and thought he might choke.

For the next several years, William went from one job to another, always earning money to hand over to his master. Once, William was hired out to a Mr. Walker, a slave driver—or, as the slaves called him, a "soul driver."[3] Walker transported slaves on the steamboat *Enterprise*, down the Mississippi River to New Orleans. It fell to William to act as steward and help the captain deliver "his cargo of human flesh."[4] When they reached New Orleans, William watched as the slaves were placed in a pen—a fenced yard where they were exhibited and auctioned. William wanted desperately to leave Walker's service, but he had no other recourse. Instead he grew more and more heartsick as he was asked to do increasingly demeaning tasks—plucking the gray hairs from old men's whiskers so they would appear younger and attract a higher price.

During the year that William worked for Walker, he made several trips to New Orleans, each time witnessing horrid abuses to the men, women, and children held captive on the boat. At the end of the year, William's master told him that he would need to sell him. He advised William to go into the city of St. Louis and look for "a good master" who could purchase him for five hundred dollars. But William made other plans. He gathered some dried beef, crackers, and cheese and left the

This image, taken between 1861 and 1869, shows the interior of a slave pen in Alexandria, Virginia. Slave dealers kept slaves in pens before selling them at auction.

city at dark, accompanied by his mother. The two found a skiff to carry them across the Mississippi River to Illinois, a free state; then they walked through the woods until day broke. Hoping they would not be captured, they remained in hiding until nightfall when, as William later recalled, "we started again on our gloomy way, having no guide but the North Star."[5]

They kept walking, even through heavy rain. On the tenth day, they stopped at a farmhouse where the people treated them kindly and gave them provisions. They set out the next morning, but within only a few hours three men on horseback accosted them. These men carried with them a handbill offering a reward for their return. Eager to collect, they captured William and his mother and put them in a wagon. Four days later, they arrived in St. Louis where they were thrown in jail.

Soon after his release, William was sold to Captain Price, a steamboat owner. When William learned that his boat was headed for Cincinnati, a city in Ohio, which was a free state, he once again dreamt of freedom and started to devise a scheme. He began by making a bag in which to store provisions. When the boat landed in Ohio, William unloaded the cargo Captain Price was delivering, then walked up the wharf, and never looked back.

William hid in the woods until nightfall, waiting for the North Star to emerge. At first it was hidden by clouds. When it appeared at midnight, William set out

by foot. He later recalled, "I suffered intensely from the cold; being without an overcoat, and my other clothes rather thin for the season."[6] He journeyed twenty or twenty-five miles the first night and continued on for several days. He found corn to eat and one night slept in a barn to stay out of the cold. He then encountered a man dressed like a Quaker in a broad-brimmed hat and a long coat. The man told William that the people who lived in the area were proslavery. Although Ohio was a free state, he said William had best stay out of sight. The man left him, promising to return.

SOURCE DOCUMENT

$100 REWARD!

RANAWAY

From the undersigned, living on Current River, about twelve miles above Doniphan, in Ripley County, Mo., on 2nd of March, 1860, A NEGRO MAN, about 30 years old, weighs about 160 pounds; high forehead, with a scar on it; had on brown pants and coat very much worn, and an old black wool hat; shoes size No. 11.

The above reward will be given to any person who may apprehend this said negro out of the State; and fifty dollars if apprehended in this State outside of Ripley county, or $25 if taken in Ripley county. **APOS TUCKER.**

Wanted posters offering rewards were often posted to entice people to turn in runaway slaves.

The wait made William nervous, but the stranger did reappear, this time in a covered wagon. He took William back to his home where he and his wife gave him food and shelter. After two weeks in their house, William was ready to move on. But first his Quaker friend, Wells Brown, asked him if he had a name besides William. When he answered no, Wells Brown said he could take his name. William accepted the name he would keep for the rest of his life—becoming William Wells Brown.

William intended to cross Lake Erie, but as soon as he reached Cleveland, he discovered that the lake was frozen. He then took a job as a waiter at an establishment called the Mansion House for twelve dollars a month. When the weather permitted, William left the Mansion House to work on a steamboat. It was then that he

William Wells Brown escaped from slavery and then helped provide transportation for other fugitives. Later, he became well known for his antislavery lectures and writings, and inspired many more to seek their freedom.

started to help transport fugitives to Canada, the place they called "the promised land."

Of the many men and women who were part of the Underground Railroad some, like William Wells Brown, have become well known, while others have remained anonymous. But all had tremendous courage and intense determination. Reading the stories of their lives opens our eyes to an amazing chapter in this country's history. The dangerous risks the fugitives took are no less surprising than the strength of the teamwork they encountered in their flights.

LIVING IN SLAVERY

In the fifteenth century, European traders first landed in West Africa, intent on turning men, women, and children into slaves who would perform hard labor in their colonies. The Europeans arrived in ships laden with rum, gunpowder, firearms, cloth, and tools and traveled inland to exchange their goods for slaves. The slave hunters took all the men and women prisoners, chained them one to the other, and forced them to march back to the coast. There the captives underwent a physical examination. The traders abandoned the weak and unhealthy and branded those they planned to sell with a hot iron.

As they waited to be sent across the ocean, the captives remained locked in the dungeons of European-built fortresses, many of which are still standing. Today visitors to the Elmina castle, built in Ghana by the Portuguese in 1482, can see these dungeons. One such visitor, Donald Jones, commented, "When I saw where they kept black women, black children, black men, the rage I felt was incomprehensible. It shook me to the core. You could still feel the dankness, and the stench still lingered."[1] Memories linger as well.

Over the course of the next two centuries, the Portuguese, Dutch, British, Spanish, and French all took part in the slave trade. They crammed as many slaves as they could onto ships, allowing them half the space they allotted convicts.[2] Some ships carried sixty slaves, others as many as six or seven hundred.[3] With little space to breathe, no room to stand, so cramped that they had to remain in one position, the slaves endured one abuse after another for the six to ten-week passage. Illnesses quickly became epidemic. Captives suffered from dysentery, from which many died, while others died from smallpox, measles, or other contagious diseases.

The captives slept on bare floors with no covering. The men were chained two by two and the women and children were generally left unchained. Twice a day the slaves were fed boiled rice or cornmeal, a cup of water, occasionally salted beef, and sometimes vegetables and fruits, such as yams, manioc, or plantains.[4] Pregnant women, with no room for privacy, gave birth to babies who, if they survived, would inherit a future doomed to slavery.

In a narrative of his life, Gustavus Vassa, a slave captured in Benin—now part of Nigeria—writes that he was placed below the decks where "with the loathsomeness of the stench, and crying together, I became so sick and low that I was not able to eat, nor had I the least desire to taste anything. I now wished for the last friend, death, to relieve me." When two white men offered him food,

he refused, provoking their anger. "One of them held me fast by the hands, and laid me across, I think, the windlass, and tied my feet, while the other flogged me severely."[5]

In 1619, the first slaves arrived in the British North American colonies. A Dutch vessel brought twenty Africans to Jamestown, Virginia, where the captain traded them for food. These slaves were treated as indentured servants—persons who contracted to serve a master in America for a period of time, usually four to seven years, in return for the ocean passage, as well as room and board. Indentured servants could be sold from one master to another, but after the predetermined number of years they would be granted their freedom. Midway through the seventeenth century, however, African slaves lost their rights as indentured servants. They were no longer granted their liberty after a predetermined number of years. Their children would never know the benefits of freedom.

After 1619, the number of slaves brought to North American shores multiplied. Virginia, South Carolina, and Georgia received the most, from both the British West Indies and Africa. In 1672, King Charles II of England chartered the Royal African Company, which became one of the largest slave trading companies in the world. By 1708, Virginia's population included twelve thousand African Americans and eighteen thousand whites. Between 1710 and 1718, 164 ships brought

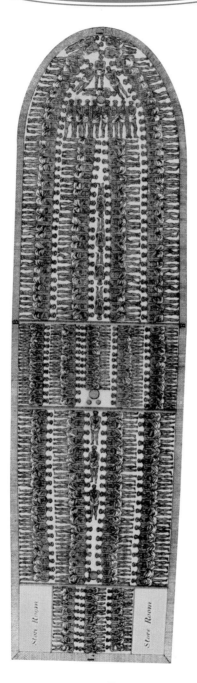

Hundreds of African captives were loaded onto each slave ship and forced to lie side by side with no room to move and little space to breathe.

4,528 additional slaves to Virginia.[6] At the start of the American Revolution the state's population was evenly divided between African-American and white persons.[7]

Slavery in the South

The increase in the number of slaves throughout the South made it possible to run large tobacco and rice plantations. The cotton grown along the coast of Georgia and South Carolina had long fibers that could easily be separated from the seeds. But the cotton produced farther inland, in a less moist climate, had shorter fibers that stuck to the seeds, making it difficult to clean. In 1793, Eli Whitney developed a new machine that could remove the seeds from the cotton. Called the cotton gin, this invention allowed for the cultivation of cotton on a grander scale. The increasingly prosperous cotton business transformed the economic status of the South. But it was not just the cotton gin that made this possible—it was the exploitation of slaves.

Most slaves left their quarters at dawn and did not return until after dark. A letter from a Virginia planter tells that a master would provide his slaves with food, typically twelve quarts of Indian meal, seven salted herrings, and two pounds of smoked bacon every week.[8] Others received what was considered a "good" allowance of a bushel of cornmeal and sixteen pounds of hog meat every month, in addition to rye coffee sweetened with molasses.[9] The masters also furnished

A new invention called the cotton gin allowed for cotton cultivation on a grand scale. The increasingly prosperous cotton business transformed the economic status of the South. But it was not just the cotton gin that made this possible—it was the exploitation of slaves.

clothing—for men, "trousers of strong cloth," three shirts, shoes and socks, one pair of summer pantaloons, a hat every second year, and every third year a winter coat and blanket. They gave the women long capes instead of coats and handkerchiefs to use as hats.[10]

Slaves were forced to submit to codes written by state legislatures. Louisiana's code, similar to the one in most Southern states, read in part:

> The condition of the slave being merely a passive one, his subordination to his master and to all who represent him is not susceptible of modification or restriction. . . . He owes to his master, and to all his family, a respect without bounds, and an absolute obedience, and he is consequently to execute all the orders which he receives from him, his said master, or from them.[11]

The codes prohibited slaves from leaving the master's property without a pass. They also were not allowed to gather in groups of more than five, practice medicine, own guns, raise animals, or testify against whites.

Slaves could preach but only in the presence of whites. They often attended churches presided over by white preachers. One ex-slave, Cornelius Garner, born in 1846, recalled in an interview recorded in dialect and later published, "De preaching us got 'twon't nothing much. Dat ole white preacher jest was telling us slaves to be good to our marsters. We ain't keer'd a bit 'bout dat stuff he was telling us 'cause we wanted to sing, pray, and serve God in our own way."[12]

Charles Thompson of Richmond, when asked if the preaching he heard was the true Gospel, answered, "One part of it, and one part burnt me as bad as ever insult did. . . . All they want you to know, is to have sense enough to say master and mistress, and run like lightning, when they speak to you, to do exactly what they want you to do."[13]

With the exception of those in Maryland, Kentucky, and the city of Washington, slaves were not legally allowed to learn to read or write. Reuben Saunders of Greene County, Georgia, remarked, "I never saw but one slave in Georgia, who could read and write, and he was brought in from another State."[14] A woman from the eastern shore of Maryland, Mrs. James Seward, reflected, "I was never sent to school, nor allowed to go to church. They were afraid we would have more sense than they."[15]

Punishment for breaking the codes was severe and flogging a common occurrence. John Warren from Tennessee recalled, "I have seen a man receive five hundred and fifty lashes for running away. The overseer and boss drank brandy, and went at him."[16] Many slaves never lost the scars that marred their bodies. Judges imposed the death penalty on slaves who committed not only murder, but robbery, arson, and rebellion, and on whites who assisted slaves in rebellion.[17]

Although slaves could live together as husband and wife, their marriage contracts were not considered

SOURCE DOCUMENT

This image, taken by Timothy O'Sullivan in the early 1860s, shows a family of slaves living on the J.J. Smith plantation in Beaufort, South Carolina.

22

valid or legal. When selling slaves, the master frequently separated a husband from a wife, a parent from a child. In a narrative of his life, a slave named James Curry said: "The separation of the slaves in this way is little thought of. A few masters regard their union as sacred, but where one does, a hundred care nothing about it."[18] One slave so feared being sold and thus separated from his family that he cut off the fingers of his left hand with an ax to make himself undesirable.[19] Slave owners expected mothers of newborn infants to return to work a week after giving birth. Field hands were made to leave their babies unattended in the shade and were only allowed to hold and feed them twice a day. One woman reported returning to her baby son only to find a large snake curled around his body. She vowed at that moment to seek freedom for herself and her child.[20]

By 1820, the number of people held in bondage in the South had reached 1,519,017, and by 1860 the number had risen to almost 4 million. Two hundred fifty thousand free African Americans were also counted. The South's white population numbered over 8 million, but only one fourth of that number owned slaves. Fewer than three thousand whites owned more than one hundred slaves. Yet slave owners controlled the political climate of the times, as well as the fate of millions of African-American men and women.[21]

Slavery in the North

In the North, slavery had followed a different course. At the end of the seventeenth century and throughout much of the eighteenth, slaves, many fewer in number than in the South, worked on farms, tending sheep and cattle and raising crops. Those in cities served their masters as carpenters, tailors, cabinetmakers, bakers, and blacksmiths. Although these slaves learned to read and write, were trained in various skills, and were allowed to marry, they could still be subject to the same abuses by their masters as the slaves farther south—mistreatment, flogging, and cruelty.

Some historians contend that there were fewer slaves in the North because slavery was not financially profitable for Northerners. Lacking the huge plantations common in the South, they did not reap the same rewards as their Southern counterparts. Yet other historians challenge this view, saying that the revolutionary spirit during the War of Independence helped sway public opinion and arouse antislavery sentiment. Vermont freed its slaves during the American Revolution through the constitution it adopted in 1777. Pennsylvania similarly passed laws to abolish slavery.

With the birth of the new country, many Americans, proud of their newly won independence, saw the injustice in withholding freedom from the African Americans, a great number of whom had fought in the revolution. In 1783, in the case of Quork Walker,

a slave who had been denied the freedom he was promised, the Massachusetts Supreme Court declared that the "idea of slavery is inconsistent with our own conduct and Constitution" and so put an end to slavery throughout Massachusetts. Other Northern states soon followed suit with state constitutions, laws, or judicial decisions.[22]

The free blacks in the North, still subject to prejudice and hostility, were not given the same educational and job opportunities as whites. They were frequently not welcome to dine or socialize with whites, and in free states outside New England they were not allowed to vote. Whites also customarily discouraged interracial marriages.[23]

Antislavery Sentiment

Beginning in the seventeenth century, many members of both races took a strong stand against slavery. In 1652, a group of New England Quakers issued a resolution against slavery, stating that "black mankind" must not be forced "to serve any man or his assignees longer than ten years," in other words, that they should be given the rights of indentured servants.[24] Another religious sect, the Mennonites, passed an antislavery resolution in 1688 in Germantown, Pennsylvania. In 1758, at the insistence of Quaker leader John Woolman, Friends—as Quakers were called—from the Philadelphia yearly meeting voted to

exclude slaveholders. Yearly meetings in New York, New England, Baltimore, Virginia, and North Carolina soon did the same.

With the start of the American Revolution came the first attempts to organize opposition to slavery. In 1775, a group of Quakers founded The Pennsylvania Society for Promoting the Abolition of Slavery, the Relief of Negroes Unlawfully Held in Bondage, and for Improving the Condition of the African Race. Within a few years, members of other religious denominations joined the society. Abolitionists—people who wanted to end slavery—followed this example and organized their own societies in several other states. In 1794, they banded together into the American Convention for Promoting the Abolition of Slavery and Improving the Condition of the African Race.

A Quaker leader and teacher, Anthony Benezet, author of several antislavery tracts (or pamphlets), profoundly influenced John Wesley, founder of the Methodist church. In 1789, his church formally prohibited its members from "buying or selling the bodies or souls of men, women, or children, with an intention to enslave them."[25] In 1816, the General Conference of the Methodist Church agreed that "no slaveholder shall be eligible to any official station in our Church hereafter, where the laws of the state in which he lives will admit of emancipation, and permit the liberated slave to enjoy freedom."[26]

The Presbyterian Church played an active role as well, declaring slavery "inconsistent with the law of God and totally irreconcilable with the gospel of Christ." The issue of slavery, however, so divided the church that in 1847 it split into a "New School" and an "Old School." The New School founded the Free Presbyterian Church in Ripley, Ohio, where antislavery feeling was vehement. By 1860, the new church had spread west into Iowa.[27]

Several slave insurrections, although unsuccessful in liberating the slaves, served to rouse public awareness of slavery. On August 30, 1800, only a storm prevented Gabriel Prosser and a band of a thousand slaves from attacking Richmond, Virginia. Prosser and fifteen followers were later hanged. In 1822, Denmark Vesey planned a slave revolt in Charleston, South Carolina; premature discovery of the plot, however, led to the hanging of thirty-six conspirators. Nat Turner, in August 1831, led a bloody slave revolt in Southampton County, Virginia, followed by the killing or capture of the rebellious slaves. Six weeks later, Nat Turner was captured and hanged.

Abolitionists

Abolitionists often promoted their cause through newspapers and tracts that they distributed as widely as possible. In 1829, a free African American, David Walker, who ran a secondhand clothing shop in Boston, published

William Lloyd Garrison's message came through loud and clear: Slavery must be stopped immediately.

a seventy-six-page antislavery pamphlet, "An Appeal to the Colored People of the World." He urged the slaves to rebel, for "the day is fast approaching, when there will be a greater time on the continent of America, than ever was witnessed upon this earth, since it came from the hand of its Creator."[28] Three editions of the pamphlet were published before the author's death in 1830. As copies of the "Appeal" reached slave states, Southern whites began to fear the power of free blacks and curtailed their rights.

On January 1, 1831, William Lloyd Garrison, a white abolitionist with a fiery tongue, published the first issue of *The Liberator*, calling for the universal emancipation of the slave. With James Forten, a successful African-American sail-maker, as its chief financial contributor and promoter, the newspaper quickly gained popularity in the African-American community. For the first few years most of the paper's subscribers were African-American. *The Liberator* remained an instrumental voice of the abolitionist cause until it folded in 1865 at the end of the Civil War.

On December 4, 1833, William Lloyd Garrison met in Philadelphia with sixty-three delegates from eleven states to form the American Anti-Slavery Society. They adopted a constitution that stated in no uncertain terms that its members owed it "to the oppressed, to our fellow-citizens who hold slaves, to our whole country, to posterity, and to God, to do all that is lawfully in our

power to bring about the extinction of slavery."[29] Women were permitted to attend the meeting but not to sign the Society's petition.

A few days later, as a result of this exclusion, Lucretia Mott, an outspoken Quaker woman, banded African-American and white women together to form the Female Anti-Slavery Society. This organization sponsored antislavery lectures, organized fairs to raise money for printing pamphlets, and started schools for African-American children. Over the next few years, women in other states founded their own societies; in 1837 they held the first Anti-Slavery Convention of American Women. African Americans ten to twenty years old created their own juvenile antislavery societies in several cities, including Boston, Pittsburgh, and

Frederick Douglass was the leading black abolitionist in the country. He was a former slave who had run away to the North.

Providence, Rhode Island. They collected dues to pay for antislavery publications and some gave concerts at abolitionist gatherings.[30]

By 1840, local antislavery societies numbered 1,006.[31] On June 12 of that year, five hundred delegates, many of them Americans from local societies, gathered in London to attend the World Anti-Slavery Convention. There they discussed the conditions of slaves and the role of churches in ending slavery. They also honored the president of the society, the stately eighty-year-old Thomas Clarkson, who had fought hard to abolish the British slave trade. His daughter-in-law passed out mementos—locks of his hair—which delegates later took back to the United States.[32] After the convention Clarkson wrote "A Letter to the Clergy of Various Denominations, and to the Slave-Holding Planters, in the Southern parts of the United States of America," in which he urged churches to take a more vehement stand against slavery.

Also attending the convention was Frederick Douglass, a fugitive from slavery who had become a prominent abolitionist and orator. He commanded the spotlight and energized the crowd every time he spoke out against slavery. Elizabeth Cady Stanton, the women's rights advocate, remembered her first encounter with Douglass: "He stood there like an African prince, majestic in his wrath, as with wit, satire and indignation he graphically described the bitterness of slavery and the humiliation of subjection."[33]

Frederick Douglass returned to the United States to continue fighting slavery. In 1847, he published the first issue of his own abolitionist newspaper, the *North Star*,

SOURCE DOCUMENT

declaring that "he who has endured the cruel pangs of Slavery is the man to advocate Liberty. It is evident we must be our own representatives and advocates—not exclusively, but peculiarly—not distinct from, but in connection with our white friends."[34]

Proslavery advocates made enemies of abolitionist newspaper publishers, taking every opportunity to close down their papers. After a band of men threw the presses for the *Cincinnati Philanthropist*, the first antislavery journal in the West, into the river for a second time, its publisher, Gamaliel Bailey, moved to Washington, D.C., to start the abolitionist *National Era*. On June 5, 1851, this paper printed the first installment of *Uncle Tom's Cabin*. The author, Harriet Beecher Stowe, continued with weekly installments, the last one appearing on April 1, 1852. Her book was then printed in its entirety, selling three thousand

*A scene from **Uncle Tom's Cabin**. The hero of the book is Eliza, a slave woman who escapes to freedom while carrying her baby in her arms. The book was read by thousands of Northerners and brought many over to the antislavery side.*

copies on the first day of publication and more than three hundred thousand during the first year.[35] The book told the story of both Eliza, a slave who escapes from Kentucky, and Uncle Tom, a slave sold to a dealer in New Orleans and subject to the cruel whims of his master. The novel captured the pathos in the lives of both slave and fugitive and gave readers a firsthand impression of the Underground Railroad.

Harriet Beecher Stowe's interest and knowledge came from years spent in Cincinnati, a border town, where she had experienced two diametrically opposed worlds. On one side of the Ohio River lay Kentucky, home to slave and slaveholder; on the other side was Ohio, a haven to slaves making their escape. *Uncle Tom's Cabin* may have converted a fair number of readers to the antislavery cause, but equally important, it served as a call to action for many who, though they opposed slavery, had previously remained passive. Readers, stirred to make their voices heard and intensify their efforts to free the slaves, supported antislavery societies with increased vigor and opened their doors to fugitives on their way North. The novel strengthened the public's awareness of the Underground Railroad, a significant, dramatic movement that would change the course of history.

3

THE FLIGHT

The first record of what was to become the Underground Railroad dates back to a letter from General George Washington, on May 12, 1786. From his home at Mount Vernon, Virginia, where Washington then owned 105 slaves, he wrote, "a society of Quakers in the city, formed for such purposes, have attempted to liberate" a slave who escaped to Philadelphia from Alexandria. In another letter written on November 20 of that year, Washington, referring to an escaped slave, said it might not be easy to apprehend him "when there are numbers who would rather facilitate the escape of slaves than apprehend them when runaways."[1] The slaves who escaped and those who came to their aid did not often leave written accounts with specific details of their activities. They preferred to keep their deeds hidden and their identities anonymous. Records now available, however, have led historians to conclude that organized assistance to runaway slaves grew steadily during the nineteenth century until the outbreak of the Civil War.

Wilbur Siebert, a history professor at Ohio State University, published *The Underground Railroad from Slavery to Freedom* in 1898 after extensive interviews with men and women who had once "traveled" on the Underground Railroad. He writes that before the term "Underground Railroad" became popular, the words "Underground Road" were used. The first known reference to this term can be traced to the year 1831. A slave named Tice Davids escaped from Kentucky into Ohio by swimming across the Ohio River. When his master, who was following close behind, got to the river he hesitated and made the fateful decision not to jump in after his slave. By the time the master found a boat to use, Tice Davids had gained a great distance. His master saw him reach the riverbank, but then lost

George Washington (foreground, second from left) is shown with some of his slaves who are harvesting grain in this idealized painting.

sight of him. He went into the nearest town to ask if there had been any sightings but was told nothing. He soon concluded that Tice Davids must have escaped on "an underground road."[2]

Although fugitives did not usually escape by train, the term "Underground Railroad" soon caught on. One term led to another—the fugitive slaves became the "passengers"; the road they traveled was the "line." Those who helped along the way were "agents" and the ones who guided the passengers to freedom were dubbed "conductors." The men and women who opened up their homes to the passengers and provided a bed, food, and often articles of clothing were called "station keepers."

Jane Pyatt, an ex-slave from Portsmouth, Virginia, born in 1848, recalled an old brick building on North Street where one could gain access to an underground tunnel that she called "an underground railroad." "This passage way," she explained,

> extended to the ferry of the Elizabeth River. Boats stayed there all the time, making it possible for many slaves to escape. Men, women and children would pack their clothes during the day and escape at night through this underground railroad.[3]

Methods of Escape

Most slaves traveled at night when the dark could offer them some measure of protection. Knowledge of the physical terrain came by word of mouth. A riverbank could serve as a marker or a distant lake would become a

much-welcomed landmark. On a clear night, many looked to the North Star for guidance. But when the clouds hid the stars, the fugitives felt the trees with their hands, knowing that moss grows longest on the north sides of trees.[4] They often had to scavenge for food, picking berries, cucumbers, or whatever else they could find. So that they would have to carry as little as possible, those who had clothes wore them in layers. Others suffered from the cold. One man lost two toes from his right foot due to frostbite. Fugitives quickly learned tricks of the trade—many changed their names while on the run and some rubbed the soles of their shoes with a red onion or spruce pine to lead astray the hounds that pursued them.[5]

An escape plan most often involved more than one means of transportation: covered wagons, carriages, and farm wagons, as well as a variety of boats and even steam trains. Fugitives hid in freight cars, and at times they were even given regular tickets on train lines through Ohio, Indiana, Illinois, New York, and Pennsylvania. Many also traveled by foot and some lucky ones by horseback. Agents who accompanied them easily devised excuses for travel. One might need to take a wagon into town to sell vegetables or another wagon might be carrying tools. Using the vegetables or tools as a cover, the agents transported fugitives—a few miles at a time—farther North.

Fugitives and their agents worked together to make the Underground Railroad run smoothly, inventing plots ranging from the simple to the extremely complex.

They developed their own codes of certain knocks and passwords that station keepers could recognize. The furtive whisper of the words "William Penn" frequently opened doors.[6] Spirituals, often sung by fugitives on the run, provided no small measure of comfort. Many of the lyrics carried double meanings, which served as a call to others to protect or join the fugitives. Passengers often wore elaborate disguises provided by sewing circles of women's antislavery societies.

For many, the joy of reaching freedom was counteracted by the pain of separation from loved ones. Many traveled alone with hopes of sending for their family later. But sometimes word of the fugitive's whereabouts never reached the family, or if it did, the journey might prove perilous for those who followed. Some families were never reunited. Isaac Forman, who escaped from Richmond to Toronto, wrote, "I can say I once was happy, but never will be again, until I see her; because what is freedom to me, when I know that my wife is in slavery?"[7]

Fugitive Slave Laws

When the Underground Railroad first got underway, and for many years after its inception, fugitives felt safe once they reached free states in the North. Passing into a free state provided a promise of security. Although the Fugitive Slave Law of 1793 gave the owner or his representative the right to seize suspected fugitives in

any state, the law was largely ignored. In fact, several states had passed laws forbidding government officials to assist in the capture of fugitives. This climate changed dramatically, however, with the passage of the Fugitive Slave Law of 1850. Those who had come to the aid of fugitives suddenly felt threatened by the possibility of arrest, heavy fines, or imprisonment.

Tension between the North and South on slavery issues had mounted over the years. Southern states were now threatening to leave the Union, and the possibility of war was discussed. Henry Clay, a longtime statesman, now a seventy-three-year-old senator from Kentucky, engineered the Compromise of 1850. As a result, the slave trade was abolished in the city of Washington, D.C., (though slavery remained); California was admitted as a free state; the inhabitants of the New Mexico and Utah territories were to make their own decision about slavery; and a new fugitive slave law would be enacted. Under this new law no one would be allowed to aid a fugitive, the fugitive would not be permitted to testify, and an affidavit by the person claiming the slave was all that was necessary to prove ownership. The refusal of a United States marshal or deputy to produce a certificate for the return of a fugitive slave would result in a one-thousand-dollar fine. If the fugitive were to escape after an arrest was made, the marshal would be liable for the value of the slave. This stringent law enraged Northerners; many of them became more willing than ever to aid the fugitives.

Oberlin College was a coeducational, racially integrated institution unique for its open admission policy. Its presence in Ohio had a significant effect on Underground Railroad activity in the area south of Cleveland. Fugitives who made it as far north as Oberlin could be assured a safe future. "Not one was ever finally taken back to bondage," said James Fairchild, president of Oberlin College.[10] The first record of Underground Railroad activity dates back to 1837, four years after the college opened: Martin L. Brooks, a graduate of the college, left Oberlin transporting in a covered wagon four fugitives on their way to Canada.

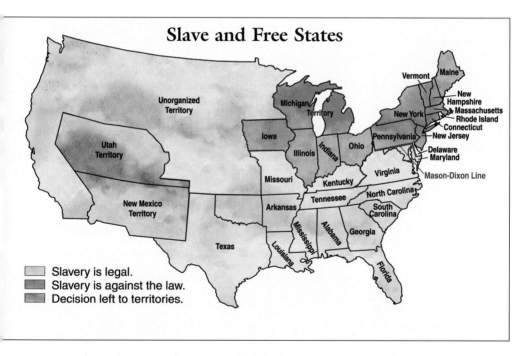

Slave and Free States

Vermont, Maine, New Hampshire, Massachusetts, Rhode Island, Connecticut, New Jersey, New York, Pennsylvania, Delaware, Maryland, Mason-Dixon Line, Michigan Territory, Unorganized Territory, Utah Territory, New Mexico Territory, Iowa, Illinois, Indiana, Ohio, Missouri, Kentucky, Virginia, North Carolina, South Carolina, Tennessee, Arkansas, Mississippi, Alabama, Georgia, Texas, Louisiana, Florida

Slavery is legal.
Slavery is against the law.
Decision left to territories.

By the early 1800s, slavery was abolished in all states north of the border of Pennsylvania and Maryland. Trouble was growing between the slave owners of the South and the abolitionists of the North.

Farther west, escape routes through Indiana and Illinois opened up in 1820. Fugitives who reached Indiana passed through Michigan, and then into Canada; those who made it to Illinois escaped by land into Wisconsin or by boat across Lake Michigan. One Underground Railroad operator from Chicago, Philo Carpenter, arranged boat passage for more than two hundred fugitives.[11] Initially many lines followed the rivers and their tributaries; later the Illinois Central Railroad, connecting Chester and Chicago, offered another means of flight.

One of the longest lines on the Underground Railroad took escaped slaves through Iowa. In 1894, Professor F. L. Parker, professor at Grinnell College in Iowa, wrote to Ohio State University professor Wilbur Siebert, who was then researching the Underground Railroad, "Along this line Quakers and Oberlin students were the chief namable groups whose houses were open to such travellers more certainly than to white men."[12]

In the East, one early line took passengers in a direct route from Washington to New York City and then to Albany. From there many escaped slaves went on to Canada through Syracuse and Rochester. The great abolitionist Frederick Douglass recalled the names of those most closely associated with each station:

Fugitives were received in Philadelphia by William Still, by him sent to New York, where they were cared for by Mr. David Ruggles, and afterwards by Mr. Gibbs, . . . thence to

Stephen Myers at Albany; thence to J. W. Loguen, Syracuse; thence to Frederick Douglass, Rochester; and thence to Hiram Wilson, St. Catherines, Canada West.[13]

Alternatively, fugitives made their way from Albany into the New England states and on to Canada. Others traveled north by ship along the Atlantic coast to New Haven, New Bedford, Boston, or Portland. From there they caught up with various land routes; many followed the Connecticut River Valley north to Vermont. From Boston some lines led through New Hampshire while others followed the coast of Maine. Those who reached Portland by ship found several families who opened up their homes, among them the Dennetts, the Winslows, and the Fessendens.

The Southern state most active in the Underground Railroad was North Carolina. Quakers who lived in Guilford County in the western part of the state joined the Underground Railroad as did Quakers in Hertford and Bertie counties, close to the coast. The town of Winton in Hertford County became a headquarters for the Underground Railroad. Fugitives would go by boat down the Chowan River to Albemarle Sound and then up the coast. The Reverend C. W. B. Gordon, an ex-slave, explained:

> They didn't allow slavery in Hertford County and [that] made everybody free if they could get across the line. . . . Underground Railroad was simply a scheme so anybody who wanted to go to Ohio, a free state, went from Winton by the hands of the Quakers. Generally, they would ship slaves on boats.[14]

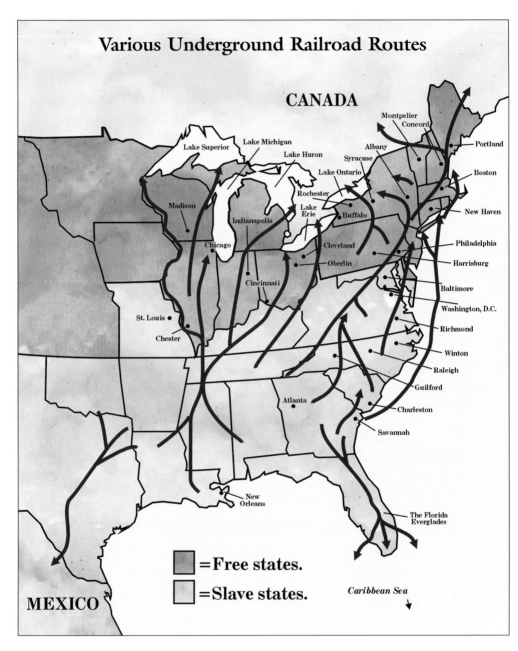

Various Underground Railroad Routes

CANADA

Montpelier
Concord
Portland
Albany
Syracuse
Boston
Lake Superior
Lake Michigan
Lake Huron
Lake Ontario
Rochester
New Haven
Madison
Indianapolis
Lake Erie
Buffalo
Chicago
Cleveland
Philadelphia
Oberlin
Harrisburg
Cincinnati
Baltimore
Washington, D.C.
St. Louis
Richmond
Chester
Winton
Raleigh
Guilford
Atlanta
Charleston
Savannah
New Orleans
The Florida Everglades

■ =Free states.
□ =Slave states.

Caribbean Sea

MEXICO

Runaway slaves made many stops along the Underground Railroad. They traveled by foot, by wagon, or boat and even by train.

Slaves in Georgia and the Carolinas did not always head north; sometimes they escaped to Southern Florida where they were taken in by the Seminole, an American Indian Tribe. Some Africans, with their knowledge of agriculture, helped cultivate the land. Others hid in the Everglades and lived close to nature. Blacks fought alongside the American Indians in the Seminole Indian Wars (1836–1842). Many were killed or forced into Arkansas by the end of the war. Some, however, were allowed to remain in a section of the Everglades that was declared neutral territory. Others of Seminole and African heritage escaped by canoe to the Bahamas, in the Atlantic Ocean east of Florida.[15] Fugitives from the deep South also sought better opportunities out west, some ending up as far away as Mexico.

Fugitives struck out in every direction. Desperate to escape, they headed wherever they hoped to find a secure home. Their destination did not have to offer much in the way of material goods. The end of the Underground Railroad line represented freedom, and for that, fugitive slaves were willing to make great sacrifices, face difficult challenges, and take enormous risks.

THE FUGITIVES

The escape of the fugitives was more often than not shrouded in mystery. Slaves carefully guarded the names of Underground Railroad operators who had come to their aid. Since most kept no written records and many of those who did destroyed them after the passage of the Fugitive Slave Law in 1850, it has not been possible to determine the precise number of fugitives who escaped on the Underground Railroad. Estimates range from thirty thousand to one hundred thousand.[1]

The danger of being caught was so great and the punishment so severe that the courage necessary to even attempt flight was extraordinary. Robert Ellett, born into slavery in 1849, recalled in an interview given in 1937, "I've seen the white folks beat slaves unmercifully for running away. They used bloodhounds to hunt them and catch them. After they beat all the skin off the slaves' backs, they wash them down in salt and water."[2] Yet thousands of slaves, well aware of the risk, set off on remarkable journeys.

Frederick Douglass

Frederick Douglass was born in 1817 or 1818 (the exact year is unknown) on a small plantation in Tuckahoe on the eastern shore of Maryland. When he was still a baby, his mother was taken from him and made to work for a man twelve miles away. Only rarely was she able to sneak away at night to be with him. She died when he was seven years old. The following year he was sent to Baltimore to work for his owner's brother and sister-in-law, Hugh and Sophia Auld. Sophia started to teach him to read, but Hugh made her stop. Frederick continued to learn on his own, and, although he was not allowed to read in the presence of the Aulds, he obtained some help from white boys he met on the street while running errands. Reading soon opened up a new world for him and whetted his desire for liberty.[3]

Frederick Douglass did not disclose the details of his flight in the early editions of his autobiography, but in a later revision, *Life and Times of Frederick Douglass*, published in 1882, he revealed his method of escape. Douglass obtained false papers stating that he was free and on September 2, 1838, disguised as a sailor, he boarded a train in Baltimore. The conductor asked to see his papers and let him pass. Douglass stepped off the train in Philadelphia a free man. He went on to New York City where he was joined a few days later by Anna Murray, his fiancée and a free woman. On September 15, 1838, they were married by the black abolitionist, the Reverend James W. C. Pennington.

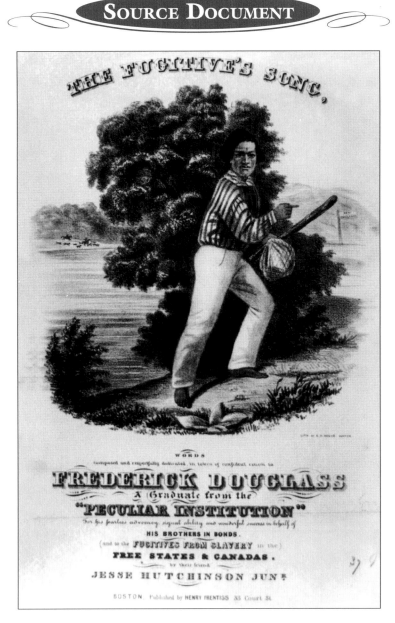

This 1845 lithograph by E.W. Bouve depicts sheet music paying tribute to Frederick Douglass, who escaped from Maryland in 1838. Douglass became the publisher of an abolitionist newspaper, the **North Star**, and one of the staunchest opponents to slavery.

Frederick Douglass became one of the greatest orators for the cause of abolition and he published an abolitionist newspaper, the *North Star*. He also opened his home in Rochester, New York, to fugitives on the Underground Railroad.

Records of William Still

While few fugitives are as famous as Frederick Douglass, many other courageous men and women also took great risks. First published in 1872, *The Underground Railroad* was written by William Still, the son of slaves and an active member of the Pennsylvania Anti-Slavery Society. The book gives firsthand accounts of intrepid fugitives who devised ingenious plots and performed daring exploits to reach freedom.

One such slave was Robert Brown, who escaped from Martinsburg, Virginia, in 1856. He traveled under the alias of Thomas Jones, carrying with him locks of hair from his wife and children. On Christmas night, he crossed the

*William Still, shown in this portrait, was the author of **The Underground Railroad**, a valuable historical record of the movement published in 1872.*

Potomac River and rode forty miles on horseback with "his wet clothing freezing to him."[4] When he had to abandon his horse because she could go no farther, he continued on foot, not reaching Philadelphia until New Year's night.

More than one slave was shipped north in a box, in this way winning freedom. Such fugitives had to remain cramped in tight positions for hours on end. One slave

THE RESURRECTION OF HENRY BOX BROWN AT PHILADELPHIA.
Who escaped from Richmond Va. in a Box 3 feet long 2½ ft deep and 2 ft wide.

This 1850 lithograph shows Henry "Box" Brown, who successfully escaped from slavery by crouching inside a shipping box for a total of twenty-six hours while traveling from Richmond to Philadelphia.

that escaped inside a box became famous. He was known as Henry "Box" Brown. In 1848, this two-hundred-pound man from Richmond, Virginia, ordered the smallest possible box to avoid arousing suspicion— one that measured two feet eight inches deep, two feet wide, and three feet long. He crawled into the box carrying only a small container of water and a few biscuits. Once inside, he could not stretch or turn, but had to remain immobile, crushed as tightly as if he were in a vise. His friend, Samuel Smith, a shoe dealer, nailed the box shut and addressed it to "Wm. H. Johnson, Arch Street, Philadelphia," and added "This side up with care." The box was sent on its way by overland express. Henry "Box" Brown traveled crouched inside the box for twenty-six hours.

At the Anti-Slavery Office in Philadelphia, preparations were made to retrieve the box. Underground Railroad agent J. M. McKim, with the help of his friend E. M. Davis, a businessperson, arranged to have a driver deliver the box to the Anti-Slavery Office. William Still, who was present at the time, recalled his arrival:

> All was quiet. The door had been safely locked. The proceedings commenced. Mr. McKim rapped quietly on the lid of the box and called out "All right!" The men used a saw and hatchet to open the box. When they lifted the lid, the marvelous resurrection of Brown ensued. Rising up in his box, he reached out his hand, saying, "How do you do, gentlemen?" . . . He was about as wet as if he had come up out of the Delaware.

The Underground Railroad agents took Brown to the home of the Quakers James and Lucretia Mott where he spent his first night as a free man.

Samuel Smith heard of his friend's successful escape and then offered his "boxing" services to two other slaves. These men, however, were apprehended and returned to slavery. Samuel Smith was arrested and sent to the penitentiary, where he stayed seven long years. When he was released, he made his way north to Philadelphia where he had not been forgotten, and he was made to feel most welcome.[5]

Harriet Jacobs

In 1861, Harriet Jacobs, a fugitive slave, published her own narrative, under the pseudonym of Linda Brent. Her autobiography, *Incidents in the Life of a Slave Girl*, was thought for a long time to be fictitious, but recent studies have shown the authenticity of her tale.[6] In 1838, Harriet Jacobs, hiding from her master, took shelter in her grandmother's attic. This garret "was only nine feet long and seven wide. The highest part was three feet high, and sloped down abruptly to the loose board floor."[7] The other inhabitants of the attic were mice, rats, and insects. The room admitted no light or air and could only be reached by a trapdoor. Harriet's grandmother, aunt, and uncle, who alone knew of her hiding place, delivered her food through the trapdoor. Eventually she was able to bore a peephole

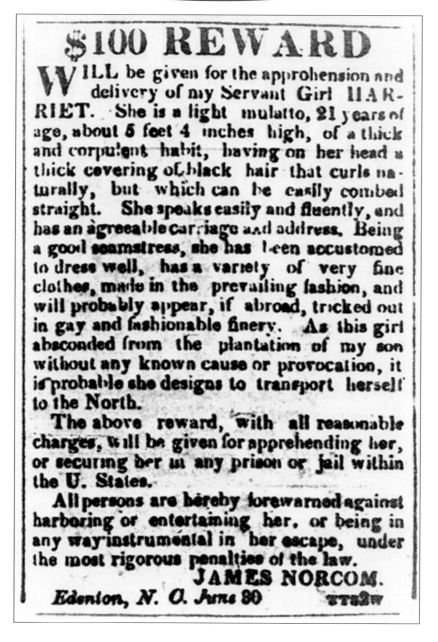

$100 REWARD

WILL be given for the apprehension and delivery of my Servant Girl HARRIET. She is a light mulatto, 21 years of age, about 5 feet 4 inches high, of a thick and corpulent habit, having on her head a thick covering of black hair that curls naturally, but which can be easily combed straight. She speaks easily and fluently, and has an agreeable carriage and address. Being a good seamstress, she has been accustomed to dress well, has a variety of very fine clothes, made in the prevailing fashion, and will probably appear, if abroad, tricked out in gay and fashionable finery. As this girl absconded from the plantation of my son without any known cause or provocation, it is probable she designs to transport herself to the North.

The above reward, with all reasonable charges, will be given for apprehending her, or securing her in any prison or jail within the U. States.

All persons are hereby forewarned against harboring or entertaining her, or being in any way instrumental in her escape, under the most rigorous penalties of the law.

JAMES NORCOM.

Edenton, N. C. June 30   ST&2w

After Harriet Jacobs escaped, her owner offered $100 for her reward.

so that she could see out onto the street. After seven years spent living in secrecy, she obtained passage on a ship that took her to New York.

William and Ellen Craft

In *Running a Thousand Miles for Freedom*, William Craft tells the story of the escape from slavery that he and his wife Ellen made in December 1848. William writes, "My wife's first master was her father, and her mother his slave."[8] This heritage accounted for Ellen's light complexion, which allowed her to pass for white. William devised a plan whereby Ellen would disguise herself as a gentleman who had taken ill and he would act as her servant. Ellen made her own trousers and William bought the other pieces of her costume. He purchased each article in a different part of town so as not to arouse suspicion.

Ellen and William, both from Macon, Georgia, obtained passes from their masters to celebrate the Christmas holiday. At this time neither Ellen nor William could read the words on their passes; they also realized Ellen would not be able to sign her name in the hotel register. Ellen soon came up with a solution. She told her husband, "I think I can make a poultice [a bandage] and bind up my right hand in a sling, and with propriety ask the officers to register my name for me."[9] The morning of their departure, William cut off Ellen's hair. She then donned her disguise, including a

pair of green spectacles. Besides the poultice on her hand, she put one on her face to hide the fact that she had no beard. She then headed for the railroad station with her "servant" in tow.

Despite all the preparations, slipping out of town was fraught with peril. William's master, by this time suspicious, arrived at the train station. He boarded the train and proceeded to check the compartments. He opened Ellen's compartment but did not recognize her. He was about to make his way into William's compartment when the train whistle blew. William's master descended the train. But more trouble lay ahead. Mr. Cray, a friend of Ellen's master who had dined with him the day before, entered Ellen's compartment. He too failed to recognize Ellen in her disguise. Fearing he would recognize her voice, Ellen pretended to be deaf.

After arriving in Savannah in the early evening, William and Ellen went to the port, where they boarded a steamer headed for Charleston. Once they arrived there, Ellen bought tickets for a steamer to Wilmington, North Carolina. After an overnight journey, they boarded a train to take them farther north. On December 24, 1848, as they changed trains in Baltimore, an officer demanded that Ellen produce papers showing that William was her slave. Both Ellen and William thought they would be discovered, thrown in prison, and returned to slavery. The conductor of

the train from Washington to Baltimore was called in to verify that they had both ridden on his train. When the bell rang for the train to leave, the officer "thrust his fingers through his hair, and in a state of great agitation said, 'I really don't know what to do; I calculate it is all right.'" Then, looking at Ellen, he told his clerk, "As he is not well, it is a pity to stop him here. We will let him go."[10]

When the train reached Havre de Grace on the Susquehanna River in northern Maryland, the first-class passengers had to leave the train and take a ferry across the river. William, who had been riding in the luggage compartment of the train, was separated from

These drawings of William and Ellen Craft appeared in William Still's *The Underground Railroad*, published in 1872. William Craft later wrote *Running a Thousand Miles to Freedom*, which describes his and his wife's escape.

Ellen on the ferry ride. Once on the other side, Ellen boarded another train but did not catch sight of William. Increasingly agitated, she inquired about his whereabouts. The conductor answered, "I haven't seen anything of him for some time: I have no doubt he has run away, and is in Philadelphia, free, long before now."[11] Ellen feared not that he had abandoned her, but that he had been kidnapped back into slavery. William, meanwhile, was safely ensconced in the luggage car of the new train on his way to Philadelphia. When a conductor later told him that Ellen was worried about him, he rushed to her side, finally putting her mind at rest.

The next morning, Christmas day, William and Ellen reached the end of their one-thousand-mile journey. They were taken to a boardinghouse where, much to the surprise of the landlord, Ellen removed her disguise. Robert Purvis, a black abolitionist, soon befriended them and introduced them to Barkley Ivens, a member of the Society of Friends. The Ivens family invited them to their home on the Delaware River. Barkley Ivens's somewhat dark complexion had convinced Ellen that he was a quadroon (a person of one quarter African-American ancestry). But when she met his wife and daughters, who looked white, she grew fearful: "I am not going to stop here; I have no confidence whatever in white people—they are only trying to get us back to slavery."[12] The Ivenses' hospitality, however, soon won Ellen over. The Quaker family fed them and sheltered them for three weeks.

Abolitionists had persuaded them not to stay in Philadelphia, but to move on to Boston for greater safety. "Public opinion in Massachusetts had become so much opposed to slavery and to kidnapping, that it was almost impossible for anyone to take a fugitive slave out of that State."[13] Once in Boston, William found employment as a cabinetmaker and Ellen as a seamstress. But, in 1850, with the passage of the Fugitive Slave Law, the Crafts' security was threatened. Two slave hunters named Hughes and Knight arrived from Macon, Georgia, in pursuit of the couple. They carried with them warrants for their arrest. No officer, however, was willing to arrest them, and instead Hughes and Knight were arrested for slander against William Craft. When they were released on bail, they were arrested again for conspiracy to kidnap and abduct William Craft. The second time they were released on bail, Hughes and Knight took no chances and departed, leaving the Crafts behind.

Even without Hughes and Knight within the city limits, the Crafts no longer felt safe in Boston. President Millard Fillmore, under pressure from the slave owners, instructed that military force be used in their arrest. The Crafts found it necessary to flee again. Abolitionists helped them reach Portland, Maine, where they planned to board a steamer for Halifax in Canada. From there they would sail to Great Britain. Once they arrived in Maine, however, they found the steamer in need of repairs. By means of coach and another steamer, they made their way

to Canadian soil and Halifax, only to discover that the steamer bound for Liverpool, England, had already departed. They were obliged to wait for another ship.

Two weeks later they boarded the *Cambria* and headed for England. What greeted them on the other side of the ocean was a freedom more complete than any they had ever known.

William Wells Brown

The first chapter traced the story of William Wells Brown, his own escape from slavery, and his efforts to help others escape. In 1843, William Wells Brown left the employment of the Lake Erie steamboat company to become a speaker for the New York Anti-Slavery Society. For many years he traveled extensively in the United States and Great Britain, giving lectures to support abolition. He carried with him original paintings showing "The Life of an American Slave," which he displayed on the walls of the various halls where he was engaged to speak.

In July 1849, William W. Brown left for Paris, France, to represent the American Peace Society at the International Peace Conference. After ten days in Paris, Brown arrived in England where he resumed the lecture circuit. While Brown was becoming a well-known lecturer, he was also making his name as a writer, with the publication of a novel, a play, and a collection of songs. Four editions of his autobiography were released in less than two years.

Brown's letters also provide a valuable record of his views and beliefs. After a visit to Oxford University in England, William Wells Brown wrote a letter to his friend Frederick Douglass, which reads in part:

> Education, though obtained by a little at a time, and that, too, over the midnight lamp, will place its owner in a position to be respected by all, even though he be black. . . . A young man once asked [Thomas] Carlyle [British thinker and author], what was the secret of success. His reply was, "Energy: whatever you undertake, do it with all your might." Had it not been for the possession of energy, I might now have been working as a servant for some brainless fellow who might be able to command my labour with his money, or I might have been yet toiling in chains and slavery.

In the same letter, William Wells Brown refers to various people he met at Oxford and adds these words:

> Then let our people take courage, and with that courage let them apply themselves to learning. A determination to excel is the secret road to greatness, and that is as open to the black man as the white. . . . It was determination that brought out the genius of a Franklin, a Fulton [American inventor], and that has distinguished many of the American statesmen, who but for their energy and determination would never have had a name beyond the precincts of their own homes. It is not always those who have the best advantages, or the greatest talents, that eventually succeed in their undertakings, but it is those who strive with untiring diligence to remove all obstacles to success, and with unconquerable resolution to labour on until the rich reward of perseverance is within their grasp.

In conclusion he writes: "Then again let me say to our young men, Take courage. 'There is a good time coming.' The darkness of the night appears greatest, just before the dawn of day. Yours, right truly, W. W. Brown."[14]

William Wells Brown's words would provide inspiration to the fugitive slaves of the pre-Civil War era, as well as to future generations of Americans looking for "the dawn of day."

5

FAMOUS CONDUCTORS

Of all the conductors on the Underground Railroad, the most well known is Harriet Tubman. She is admired for her fearlessness, ingenuity, and determination. Some might call her brazen, for she dared to undertake what others only dreamed of doing. Many never knew Harriet Tubman personally, but they knew of her. Her work was legendary and earned her the name of "Moses" for the Hebrew lawgiver who led his people out of bondage in Egypt. Robert Ellett, an ex-slave from Virginia, recollected:

> Moses would come around like today and tonight she would run them away and get them over near the border line and run them over into Pennsylvania the next night on what you call the "Underground Railroad." I never saw "Moses." I heard talk of her, but I never saw her.[1]

Harriet Tubman

Harriet Tubman was born a slave in 1820 on a plantation in Dorchester County, Maryland. In 1849, she escaped from her master Edward Brodas. The following year she returned to Baltimore to lead her sister's family north; within a few months she had rescued her brother and two others. She also managed to bring her elderly parents out of slavery. Since they could not walk long distances, she made use of an old horse and a "patched together" vehicle that consisted of a pair of wheels "with a board on the axle to sit on and another board swinging by ropes from the axles" on which her parents could rest their feet.[2] Harriet transported her parents to the train station in this unique fashion and then helped them board the train to Wilmington, Delaware.

This amazing "conductor" returned to the South nineteen times to lead more than three hundred fugitives out of slavery. Slaves learned to recognize her by the song she sang:

> Dark and thorny is the pathway,
> Where the pilgrim makes his ways;
> But beyond this vale of sorrow, Lie
> the fields of endless days.[3]

Harriet was a shrewd planner and a tough taskmaster. She would depart on a Saturday night to give the slaves more time to get away before they would be missed, since they did not work Sunday morning. She always urged her companions to press forward and would not allow anyone to lag behind. Along her route she often found friends who would offer shelter to her entire party. Whatever money she had she used to help her mission, sometimes paying people to tear down advertisements for the runaways. Many slaveholders grew to fear her and offered a forty thousand dollar reward for her capture.

Along with helping runaway slaves, Harriet Tubman was also a spy for the Union Army during the Civil War.

This "Moses of Her People" was noted for her courage, as well as her faith. The Quaker and abolitionist Thomas Garrett once said, "I never met with any person, of any color, who had more confidence in the voice of God, as spoken to her soul. She has frequently told me that she talked with God, and he talked with her, every day of her life."[4] It was a faith that allowed her to do great things.

Risks and Schemes

Conductors on the Underground Railroad needed to find ingenious ways to help their passengers, since an escape method used once too often could result in capture. George W. C. Lucas, a free black in Salem, Ohio, built a false-bottomed wagon. George L. Burroughs worked as a sleeping car porter on the railroad so he could smuggle passengers from Cairo, Illinois, to Chicago.[5]

Both fugitive and helper frequently risked imprisonment. The abolitionist Reverend Charles T. Torrey surreptitiously attended a meeting of slaveholders in Annapolis, Maryland, in 1842. He planned to report on the meeting in an antislavery newspaper, but he was recognized, caught, and put in prison. While there he devised the idea of establishing a prearranged route for the Underground Railroad (in contrast to less-organized routes already in use in that part of the country). After he was released, Reverend Torrey helped four hundred fugitives escape. Two years later, he was arrested and convicted; he died in prison soon after.[6]

Calvin Fairbank was another abolitionist forced to serve not one, but two prison terms for his work. Fairbank studied at Oberlin College where he made many friends in the antislavery movement. In 1837, he started work as a conductor on the Underground Railroad. Seven years later he was arrested in Kentucky for helping to rescue Harriet Hayden, the wife of a fugitive. He served five years of his sentence before being issued a pardon. Fairbank immediately went back to work as an Underground Railroad conductor. Thrown in jail again in 1852, he remained there until 1864, receiving, he said, a total of thirty-five thousand lashes.[7]

Despite the risks, conductors continued their work undaunted. A Quaker from Delaware, Thomas Garrett, helped twenty-seven hundred fugitives travel on the Underground Railroad. He was to serve as one of the models for the character of Simeon Halliday in Harriet Beecher Stowe's *Uncle Tom's Cabin*.[8] At the age of sixty, Thomas Garrett was brought to trial for his work in aiding

Thomas Garrett was a Quaker from Delaware who helped twenty-seven hundred slaves travel on the Underground Railroad.

fugitives. The judge sentenced him to a fine amounting to eight thousand dollars—his life's earnings—and warned him to refrain from further assistance to fugitives. Thomas Garrett answered, "Judge, thou hast not left me a dollar, but I wish to say to thee, and to all in this court-room, that if any one knows of a fugitive who wants a shelter and a friend, send him to Thomas Garrett and he will befriend him."[9]

Robert and Harriet Purvis

Born in Charleston, South Carolina, in 1810, Robert Purvis was the son of an English merchant and a free-born woman of German-Jewish and African heritage. When Robert was ten his family moved to Philadelphia. Six years later his father died, leaving him a small fortune that he successfully invested in real estate. Purvis recalled that, "in the year 1830 I became interested in anti-slavery through my acquaintance with Benjamin Lundy and William Lloyd Garrison."[10] Both abolitionists were involved in newspaper work. Lundy edited *The Genius of Universal Emancipation*, and Garrison was preparing to publish the first issue of *The Liberator*.

Another influential figure in Purvis's youth was James Forten, a prominent African-American businessperson, who was both an advisor to William Garrison and a financial contributor to *The Liberator*. Robert looked up to Forten as a father and at the same time was falling in love with his daughter Harriet. On September 13, 1831, Robert and Harriet were married. They moved to a house on Lombard

Street in Philadelphia where they started to raise a family and work together in the abolitionist movement. Purvis helped form the American Anti-Slavery Society in 1833 and signed its Declaration of Sentiments.

Purvis solicited money, as well as help, for the Underground Railroad from numerous "agents." He recalled that the most efficient were two women from Baltimore, one white and one black, who sold goods in the marketplace. They had obtained certificates of freedom or "passports," which they would give to slaves wishing to escape. These papers were later returned to the women to be reissued to other slaves.

In 1838, Purvis organized an official society of the Underground Railroad, called the Vigilance Committee, in Philadelphia:

> The fugitives were distributed among the members of the society, but most of them were received at my house in Philadelphia, where . . . I caused a place to be constructed underneath a room, which could only be entered by a trap-door in the floor.[11]

Unlike other branches of the Underground Railroad, this one was organized more formally, with an elected president, a secretary, and committee members. Robert Purvis served as president of the organization and later as chair of its successor, the General Vigilance Committee, which remained active until the abolition of slavery.

The meeting of the second Women's Anti-Slavery Convention in Philadelphia was planned in May 1838

to include both white and African-American women. It was to take place in Philadelphia's newly constructed Pennsylvania Hall, which had an auditorium that could hold three thousand. At the opening of the proceedings antiabolitionists gathered outside the hall in an attempt to disrupt the proceedings. They were disturbed by the presence of African-American women and even more angered when they saw Harriet Purvis, a black woman, step out of her carriage accompanied by her husband Robert—a man they wrongly presumed to be white. The idea of amalgamation, or the mixing of races, so offended them that a riot erupted and the hall was burned to the ground.[12]

In 1843, the Purvis family moved to a large estate in Byberry, Pennsylvania. Their house became a gathering place for abolitionists from all over the United States and Britain. Just as the Purvis home in Philadelphia had been open to fugitives, so too was the new house at Byberry. "His house was a well-known station on the Underground Rail Road,"

Robert Purvis was a prominent Philadelphia merchant and black abolitionist. He and his wife Harriet organized antislavery societies and provided shelter to thousand of fugitives.

William Still wrote. "His horses and carriages, and his personal attendance, were ever at the service of the travelers upon that road."[13]

Robert Purvis kept records of fugitives who received help from the Vigilance Committee. Although he destroyed his records after the passage of the Fugitive Slave Law in 1850, he estimated that the committee provided aid to fugitives on the average of one per day.[14] One of these fugitives, Madison Washington, returned to Virginia to rescue his wife and stopped at the Purvises along the way. But after he left their house he was captured, sold to a slave dealer, and put with other slaves onto the *Creole*, a ship bound for New Orleans, Louisiana. These passengers, however, never made it to their destination—the auction block. Washington staged a mutiny and redirected the ship to the Bahamas. The passengers stepped off the boat free men and women.

Robert and Harriet Purvis helped literally thousands of fugitives, and were highly respected members of the abolitionist community. People turned to them for both guidance and leadership. A case in point followed the arrest of John Brown. This fearless abolitionist had led a band of antislavery men in capturing the United States arsenal at Harpers Ferry, a town in the mountains of what is now West Virginia. Brown wanted to use the arsenal as a stronghold for fugitive slaves. The hanging of John Brown on December 2, 1859, rocked the nation. Robert

Purvis was the one chosen to speak to the hundreds who gathered at National Hall on Martyr Day, the day of mourning for John Brown.

Levi Coffin

Levi Coffin, a Quaker born in 1798 in New Garden, North Carolina, also earned the title of president of the Underground Railroad. Although he was never formally elected, he became known as such while running one of the most active stations on the Underground Railroad and providing shelter to fugitives for thirty-three years. At an early age, Coffin witnessed the cruelties of slavery. He remembered that at the age of seven he first saw a slave in chains. When Coffin asked why he had to wear the chains, the slave told him he had been separated from his wife and children, so his owner had chained him to prevent him from running back to them.

On his twenty-sixth birthday, October 26, 1824, Coffin married a twenty-one-year-old Quaker from New Garden named Catherine White. Coffin taught school for the first two years of their marriage. They then moved to Indiana to join Coffin's parents and his wife's brother. It took four weeks of wagon travel to reach Newport (now Fountain City), Indiana, where Coffin opened a general store.

Levi and his wife, called Kate, quickly discovered that they were on a line of the Underground Railroad, where several free black families lived. They were descendants of

slaves from North Carolina, who had been liberated by The Society of Friends and sent to Newport at the expense of the Friends' North Carolina yearly meeting. These families often took in fugitive slaves. The Coffins followed suit, offering their house as shelter. When other white families saw what was happening, many contributed clothes and money to help forward the fugitives farther north, but were reluctant to house them for fear of being caught. "Some seemed really glad to see the work go on, if somebody else would do it," Coffin wrote. "Others doubted the propriety of it, and tried to discourage me, and dissuade me from running such risks."[15] They tried to convince Coffin that this work would hurt his business, cause financial ruin, and endanger his life, as well as his family's.

Coffin did lose some of his proslavery customers, but he kept up his work on the Underground Railroad. Fugitives came from many points south of the Ohio River, from Alabama, Mississippi, and Louisiana, as well as from Kentucky and Tennessee:

> Three principal lines from the South converged at my house; one from Cincinnati, one from Madison, and one from Jeffersonville, Indiana. The roads were always in running order, the connections were good, the conductors active and zealous, and there was no lack of passengers.[16]

At night Levi and Kate were often awakened by a tap at the door. Upon opening the door, Coffin would find a two-horse wagon carrying fugitives. The parties,

varying in number from two to seventeen, would enter the house silently. Once they were inside, Levi would fasten the door, cover the windows, and light a fire. Kate would fix supper for the company and prepare pallets on the floor.

In his autobiography, Coffin wrote of one couple whose master had locked them in a room after telling them they were about to be sold. They quickly devised a plan to escape. They tied their sheets together, fastened one end to the bedpost, let the other end out the window, and hanging onto the knotted sheets, slid to the ground. The couple reached the Ohio River by foot, found a skiff, and rowed across the river. Once on the other side they went to the home of a friend, a free man who took them to the Coffins. Levi and Kate let them hide in an upstairs room for several weeks. Their master, hearing they had made it as far as Newport, pursued them, searching the town and the surrounding area. On one occasion, the couple looked out of their small window to see their master on the street below. But he never entered the Coffin house and finally left town.

Coffin then went from one proprietor to another collecting money to send the fugitives off to Canada. Each businessperson gave a dollar or two. One merchant was reluctant, but changed his mind, and following Levi out the door, handed him a silver half-dollar. A week later, when the merchant met Coffin, he whispered "Did they

get off safely?" Coffin answered, "Ah, thou hast taken stock in the Underground Railroad, and feels an interest in it; if thou hadst not taken stock thou wouldst have cared nothing about it. Yes, they got off safely, and by this time are probably in Canada."[17]

Sometimes the escaped slaves spent only one night, but, if they were exhausted or sick, they often stayed much longer. Coffin's friend, Dr. Henry H. Way, attended to their medical needs. A team of horses and a wagon were always kept for transporting fugitives. When they were ready to move on, Coffin would take them to the next depot, ten, fifteen, or twenty miles away, traveling at night, often through deep mud and over bad roads.

In 1844, Coffin read the work of Quaker leader John Woolman and determined "as a matter of conscience, to abstain so far as I could from the products of slavery, and in my business to buy and sell, so far as possible, only the products of free labor."[18] After learning that associations in Philadelphia and New York were manufacturing goods of free cotton and obtaining groceries from the British West Indies and other free countries, Coffin pledged to deal only in free-labor goods in his store in Newport. In 1846, a convention was held at the Friends' meeting house in Salem, Indiana, to discuss the issue of free labor. A resolution was passed to raise three thousand dollars as a loan to a suitable person who would open a wholesale depository

of free-labor goods in Cincinnati. Levi and Kate had no desire to move and preferred life in a small town to life in a city. But the committee chosen to find a suitable person, knowing Coffin already had experience in this area, urged him to accept the position. Eventually he relented.

The Coffins made what they thought would be a temporary move. Their reputation traveled with them and they soon found themselves once again heavily involved in Underground Railroad work. Fugitives "sometimes came to our door frightened and panting and in a destitute condition, having fled in such haste and fear that they had no time to bring any clothing except what they had on, and that was often very scant."[19] The Coffins lived in a large house with chambers upstairs where fugitives could hide. Kate brought them food in a basket, placing "a freshly ironed garment on the top to make it look like a basketful of clothes" so the other boarders or guests would not grow suspicious.[20]

Over the years more than three thousand slaves came through the Coffins' doors to receive food and shelter. Levi and Kate kept their house open to fugitives until all slaves were freed. Many of the fugitives' stories can be found in a book written by Levi Coffin and published in 1876. At the age of seventy-eight, Coffin recorded his experiences in the Underground Railroad in *Reminiscences of Levi Coffin*, which is both an exposé of cruelty and a testament to courage.

Friends of the Underground Railroad

Although they may not have worked as conductors, many others helped operate the Underground Railroad. Sojourner Truth, born into slavery in New York at the eve of the nineteenth century, was freed in 1827, shortly before the state abolished slavery. In her autobiographical narrative recorded by Olive Gilbert, she tells of a call from God to sing and preach. Starting in 1843, she took on the cause of abolition. Her commanding presence always attracted large crowds.

Maria W. Stewart, also an African-American abolitionist, was born in Hartford, Connecticut, in 1803. She spoke and wrote in opposition to slavery. Included in her autobiographical and spiritual meditations, published in 1835, is the following:

> According to the Constitution of these United States, [God] hath made all men free and equal. Then why should one worm say to another, "Keep you down there, while I sit up yonder; for I am better than thou?" It is not the color of the skin that makes the man, but it is the principles formed within the soul.[21]

She advised the African race to build their own stores and sue for rights and privileges. "Possess the spirit of independence," she urged. "You can but die, if you make the attempt; and we shall certainly die if you do not."[22]

Another woman who became a true friend of the Underground Railroad was the poet and lecturer Frances Ellen Watkins Harper, born in Baltimore to free parents in

1825. At the age of twenty-six, she moved north to Ohio and then to Pennsylvania where she discovered the Underground Railroad. Her concern for the fugitives' welfare grew—before long she was offering them food, clothing, and money. The passengers became the subject of her verse. In 1854, she gave her first lecture on "Education and the Elevation of the Colored Race." She soon attracted large audiences at lectures sponsored by antislavery societies. She spoke out on education, abolition, and the importance of free produce (or the boycott of goods produced by slave labor), while still showing a deep interest in individual passengers. In one letter to an agent of the Underground Railroad she wrote, "I see by the Cincinnati papers that you have had an attempted rescue and a failure. That is sad! Can you not give me the particulars? And if there is anything that I can do for them in money or goods, call upon me."[23]

Friends of the Underground Railroad chose diverse ways to help the fugitives. Many worked secretly, covering up the help they gave; others spoke loudly behind a podium or from a pulpit. And some, as we shall see in the following chapter, turned to the court of law to defend the slaves and those who helped them.

6

ON TRIAL

In 1848, the District of Columbia counted a population of fifty-two thousand, including ten thousand free African Americans and thirty-seven hundred slaves. Those who were free worked years and years without a single holiday to save the money that would allow them to buy the freedom of a loved one— five hundred to one thousand dollars, sometimes more, sometimes less. For many the price was too daunting; they could not imagine themselves, their friends, or relatives raising so much money. In April 1848, seventy-seven of those thirty-seven hundred slaves decided they would wait no longer to buy their liberty; neither would they remain slaves. They would break free.

Captains of the *Pearl*

News had just reached America that the French people had overthrown their king, Louis Philippe, and were in the process of forming a republic. Washington, D.C., was in a celebratory mood. While the people lit bonfires and staged torch-light processions, senators publicly acclaimed the French people's newly found freedom. But the slaves, listening in the shadow of the crowd, knew the speeches were hollow. Word began to spread among them that a plot was underway to help a group of slaves escape by boat. A boat captain named Daniel Drayton had volunteered to take the fugitives aboard the *Pearl*. He planned to sail down the Potomac River to the Chesapeake Bay, and then up to the Delaware River, and on into the free state of New Jersey.[1]

On the night of April 15, Captain Drayton, his companion Captain Sayres, and seventy-seven slaves set sail on the Potomac. The following evening, when heavy winds prevented them from rounding the bend at Point Lookout, they dropped anchor at Cornfield Harbor. Back in Washington, D.C., the slave owners formed a posse to search for the fugitives. After they learned of the plot from a hack driver who had delivered several slaves to the dock, the posse, thirty-five strong and armed with muskets, boarded a steamboat in pursuit of the *Pearl*. They surprised the *Pearl* still anchored at Cornfield Harbor, captured the unarmed fugitives, took Drayton and Sayres aboard their boat, and chained them. The posse towed the *Pearl* back to Washington, D.C., where they threw the fugitives into jail. Most of the owners refused to take the slaves back, choosing instead to sell them. The captives soon transferred from the jail to slave pens in Alexandria, Virginia, and Baltimore, Maryland, and then taken to New Orleans, Louisana, to be sold.

Drayton and Sayres, on the other hand, would stand trial. Word of their arrest quickly spread throughout antislavery circles. Charles Sumner and Samuel Gridley Howe, abolitionists from Massachusetts, urged Horace Mann, the newly elected antislavery member of Congress from Massachusetts, to represent the defense. Mann had become a leader in education and prison reform, and had traveled widely to study reforms in Europe. It had been many years since he had practiced law, but he agreed to take the case.

Philip Barton Key, the debonair United States district attorney for Washington, D.C., stood for the prosecution. He insisted the captains were guilty of two misdeeds: the first, assisting the slaves to escape, and the second, stealing them with the intent to sell them for a profit. Both crimes carried serious penalties. If found guilty of the former, they could be fined over

Daniel Drayton was the captain of the Pearl, a boat on which seventy-seven slaves attempted to flee Washington, D.C., in April 1848. He was tried and eventually convicted for assisting in their escape.

fifteen thousand dollars. If found guilty of the second crime, they could be sentenced to as many as twenty years imprisonment.

In the first trial, which involved two slaves owned by a man named Andrew Houver, the district attorney called to the stand Captain Baker, whose boat had pursued the *Pearl*. Baker testified that he had seen another ship anchored at Point Lookout that was owned by pirates. Drayton, he said, planned to hand over the slaves to the pirates who would take them to Cuba to be sold. To refute this argument, Mann called a witness who testified that Point Lookout was a popular anchorage spot and the presence of a larger ship must not lead one to assume that the slaves were to be transferred to it. Another witness stated that he had heard Drayton claim that he wanted to help the fugitives reach a free state.

"The accused cannot be guilty of two crimes," Mann told the jury. "Gentlemen, you have before you the case of a man who assisted certain slaves in escaping their master, not a man guilty of larceny." In his closing remarks Mann rejected the district attorney's contention that Drayton had enticed the slaves on board. "Might they not have gone without being enticed at all?" he asked. He then reminded the jury, "We wished to call the slaves themselves as witnesses but the law shuts up their mouths."[2]

On the day the verdict was to be handed down, the courthouse was packed with city folk. Drayton was found guilty of stealing and sentenced to spend twenty years in the

penitentiary. In a separate trial Sayres was judged to have played a lesser role in the affair, providing transportation, but not plotting to steal the slaves. He was found guilty of assisting in the escape of the slaves and sentenced to a fine of one hundred and fifty dollars for each of seventy-four indictments.

Drayton's case was appealed and tried again in the Criminal Court. This time Drayton was found not guilty of stealing Houver's slaves. Key agreed not to try the other cases if Drayton would accept guilty verdicts for assisting in the slaves' escape with terms comparable to those received by Sayres in the previous trial. The defense agreed and Drayton received a sentence with fines amounting to ten thousand and sixty dollars.

Both Drayton and Sayres, unable to pay the fines, remained in jail. In 1850, after Vice President Millard Fillmore succeeded to the presidency following the death of Zachary Taylor, he issued Drayton and Sayres an unconditional pardon. Daniel Drayton was reunited with his family and, in 1855, published his personal memoirs. Here he wrote, "If a man wishes to realize the agony which our American slave trade inflicts in the separation of families, let him personally feel that separation, as I did; let him pass four years in the Washington jail."[3] The Drayton-Sayres case, which was widely reported in abolitionist newspapers, including *The Liberator* and Washington's *National Era*, increased public outrage and provided fuel for the abolitionist movement.

The Anthony Burns Case

Another case with national repercussions involved twenty-four-year-old Anthony Burns who, in 1854, escaped from his master Charles F. Suttle of Virginia and fled to Boston. Burns wrote a letter to his brother and had it mailed from Canada, but in the letter he made reference to Boston. All mail sent to slaves was routinely opened by the master before being passed on to the slave, so Charles Suttle read the fugitive's letter and learned of his whereabouts.

Suttle had Burns arrested on May 25, 1854, and planned to take him back into slavery. But the people of Boston thought otherwise. Word of the arrest spread and the next day signs for a public meeting to be held at Faneuil Hall were posted throughout the city. Hundreds of Bostonians, shocked and angry, gathered to choose a course of action. At the Faneuil Hall meeting, Judge George Russell expressed indignation that a fugitive could be taken from Boston. He argued that those gathered together should not relent, but stand firm in their opposition to the slaveholders. "We have made compromises until we find that compromise is concession, and concession is degradation."[4]

Abolitionist Wendell Phillips told the audience:

> I don't profess courage, but I do profess this: when there is a possibility of saving a slave from the hands of those who are called officers of the law, I am ready to trample any statute or any man under my feet to do it, and am ready to help any one hundred men to do it.[5]

A portrait of the fugitive slave Anthony Burns. Burns' arrest and trial under the Fugitive Slave Act of 1850 touched off riots and protests by abolitionists and citizens of Boston in the spring of 1854. A bust portrait of the twenty-four-year-old Burns, is surrounded by scenes from his life.

He urged the audience to wait until morning before attempting a rescue, yet the crowd would not be silenced nor keep still.[6] They followed the Reverend Thomas Higginson to the courthouse and, with a beam and axes, broke through the heavy door. As the first man stepped into the courthouse, the Boston Artillery appeared and a shot was fired. Burns was not freed, but in the ensuing riot one of the United States Marshal's guards was killed.

Burns stood trial and was ordered to return to his master. President Franklin Pierce had called for a large military force to take him to the dock where he was to board the government cutter to bring him south. Police, United States troops from the Fourth Regiment Artillery, and the Marines guarded Burns as he was led through the streets of Boston. In addition, a special band of one hundred twenty officers, armed with swords and revolvers, kept close watch over Burns. The buildings they passed were draped in black and angry crowds gathered on street corners. The atmosphere was tense: One witness remarked, "It was evident that a very trifling incident might have brought on a collision, and flooded the street with blood."[7] When the procession finally reached the Commonwealth building on State Street, "a shower of cayenne pepper" or "other most noxious substance" is reported to have been thrown.[8] It was followed by a bottle containing vitriol (a sulphuric acid that would burn the skin), but no one was severely hurt.

After Burns was returned to the Suttle plantation in Virginia, abolitionists raised thirteen hundred dollars to buy his freedom. Newly liberated, he traveled to Ohio where he studied for two years at Oberlin College. He continued his education at Fairmount Theological Seminary in Cincinnati and gave lectures on slavery and abolition.

The arrest of Burns and his return to slavery are reputed to have cost the government a substantial sum—historians' estimates range from forty thousand dollars[9] to one hundred thousand dollars.[10] That such a high cost was necessary only served to demonstrate the lack of support behind the Fugitive Slave Act (which legalized the return of escaped slaves). As a result the Massachusetts legislature passed the Personal Liberty Law, nullifying the enforcement of the Fugitive Slave Act in the state. It banned the forced return of the fugitives and guaranteed their freedom.

The Oberlin-Wellington Rescue

On September 13, 1858, two slave catchers from Kentucky arrived in Oberlin. Accompanied by a United States marshal, they tracked down and captured an eighteen-year-old fugitive named John Price. The men took their captive eight miles away to the town of Wellington where they planned to board the southbound train. But two young men who had witnessed the capture spread the word at Oberlin College. A group of two hundred, including students and professors, set out

for the railway station in Wellington. They located John Price near the station in the upper story of a house where he was held prisoner. A few students obtained a ladder and engineered a rescue through the window of the building.

Thirty-seven citizens of Oberlin and Wellington were indicted and made to appear before the United States District Court in Cleveland. When two of the men were tried and convicted, public meetings were held throughout the southeastern part of Ohio to plan for their release. A "Fund of Liberty" was set up to be used for the defense of the rescuers. In Lorain County, where the fugitive was captured, a grand jury turned the tables and indicted the

This photograph shows "The Oberlin Rescuers." When two slave catchers captured John Price, an escaped slave from Kentucky, in September 1858, a group of men from Oberlin, Ohio, set out to free him from the building where he was held captive.

slave catchers. Like Massachusetts, Ohio had passed a Personal Liberty Law, which barred slave catchers from capturing a fugitive. A settlement was reached whereby the United States District Court in Cleveland would stop the prosecution of the rescuers and the Lorain County grand jury would dismiss the suits against the slave catchers. When the prisoners were released in Cleveland, one hundred guns were fired. A grand celebration took place in Oberlin upon their return.[11]

The town of Oberlin has not forgotten the Oberlin-Wellington rescue. A monument, dedicated on May 7, 1990, commemorates the rescue and is dedicated to the men who were imprisoned. The words on the plaque read:

> In the spring of 1859 twenty Oberlinians went to jail
> For the crime of rescuing John Price from slavery.
> With their comrades in the abolition cause
> They kindle hopes of freedom for us all.

7

THE PROMISED LAND

Before the passage of the Fugitive Slave Law, slaves who escaped to the North found liberty, but they soon discovered that this freedom was tainted. They often encountered difficulties in finding skilled occu-pations, were turned away at certain eating houses, and were denied admission to a number of schools and churches. Public transportation was segregated and first-class accommodations were most often refused to them. Fugitives heard they would fare better in Canada and Great Britain so they pressed on, hoping to find a less prejudiced world. Once the Fugitive Slave Law went into effect, the number of fugitives who feared recapture and wished to leave the country altogether mushroomed. Many felt they had no other choice but to leave.

Crossing the Border

Fugitives made new homes in many towns along the Canadian border. Crossing Lake Erie from Ohio, they settled in Windsor, Sandwich, Elgin, Chatham, Camden, Dawn, and Dresden. Farther north along the Thames

River they found homes in London and Wilberforce. Those who crossed Lake Ontario settled in St. Catharines, Hamilton, Brantford, and Toronto. Most fugitives escaped to these towns and settlements in what was known as Canada West and is today Ontario; others fled to Canada East, crossing overland from New England states to Quebec or by boat to New Brunswick and Nova Scotia.

Exact population figures are hard to determine, but the Anti-Slavery Society of Canada and travelers to the region have made attempts to estimate the number of fugitive settlers. Levi Coffin, on a visit to Canada in 1844, reported hearing that forty thousand fugitives had

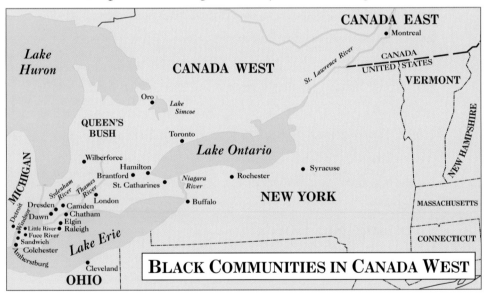

This map, adapted from **Black Abolitionist Papers** (edited by C. Peter Ripley) shows the communities in Canada West where fugitives settled. Estimates of the number of blacks who had settled in Canada West by 1855 range from fifty to sixty thousand.

reached Canada.[1] In 1852, the Anti-Slavery Society of Toronto estimated that the number of African Americans in Canada West totalled thirty thousand.[2] By 1855, the African population in all of Canada is said to have reached fifty thousand.[3] Some estimates of sixty thousand, including fifteen thousand freeborn and forty-five thousand fugitives, are also given.[4]

The British law that Canada adhered to made it possible for fugitives in Canada to purchase land at a low cost. Friends of the fugitives were able to send them supplies free of customs duty. Their children could attend local schools, some "common" (for blacks and whites) and others "separate." Jobs, although not lucrative, were available. Many of the fugitives farmed their own land or hired themselves out to do farm labor. They found themselves in great demand at a time when most of the land was still uncultivated. Those who owned property and paid taxes earned the right to vote on the same terms as other immigrants.[5]

Yet, in most cases, it took time for the fugitives to achieve adequate living conditions and a minimal level of security. In 1844, Coffin found that many of the fugitives in Canada West were:

> more comfortably situated than we expected, but there was much destitution and suffering among those who had recently come in. Many fugitives arrived weary and footsore, with their clothing in rags, having been torn by briers and bitten by dogs on their way . . .[6]

Although some escaped with family or friends, others often came alone, leaving behind loved ones.

W. P. Jacobs, born a slave in Virginia in 1852, recalls that when he was only six years old, his Uncle Charlie escaped from his master (who was also his half-brother). He slept during the day and traveled by night. Once he made it to Chicago he crossed the lake on a boat and went into Canada. He was put with a family who sent him to school. When they asked if there was anyone he particularly missed from the plantation, he told them he wanted to see the woman he loved. "Days went by and nothing happened." But one evening when he came home "he was shocked to see his Rachel at the table. Tears flooded his eyes, and he almost broke his neck by falling over a chair as he rushed to greet her." Uncle Charlie married Rachel and became a Methodist minister. He wrote his master in Virginia saying "he would be welcome to the hospitality of their home anytime he cared to call, since they had the same father." There is no record, however, of such a meeting.[7]

John Henry Hill, a Virginia slave and carpenter by trade, hired himself out and handed over his earnings to his owner John Mitchell. Finding him an "ardent lover of Liberty,"[8] Mitchell feared this young man might love liberty so much that he would run away, and so, on the first of January 1853, he took him to the auction block in Richmond with plans to have him sold. Just as the slave dealer was about to handcuff him, John fought him off—and ran.

John kept running for nine months. He passed through Philadelphia, into New York State, stopping at Albany, Rochester, and Lewiston (near Niagara Falls), and finally reached Toronto. On October 4, 1853, he wrote to William Still, "I found this to be a very handsome city. I like it better than any city I ever saw." He later wrote, "I wants you to let the whole United States know we are satisfied here because I have seen more Pleasure since I came here than I saw in the U.S. the 24 years that I served my master."[9] For John, Canada offered the promise of security; the country stood as a beacon for all ex-slaves.

But John could not enjoy his liberty until his wife and two children, who were already free, joined him. In a letter he asked William Still to give them advice on traveling to Toronto. William Still helped them prepare for the journey. They set off, but made it only as far as Niagara Falls, where John's wife realized she had lost the rest of her money. The money she had saved for the remainder of the trip was nowhere to be found. She telegraphed John on a Saturday to come pick them up at the Falls. John departed immediately after receiving the telegram, and arrived at Niagara Falls on Monday. It was a time for great rejoicing.

Yet John still was not completely satisfied. Back in Toronto, he would frequently think of friends across the border. Eager to help them, he corresponded with William Still to make arrangements for their escape. He wrote his friend that although it was true that he had to work very

hard for comfort, he was "Happy, Happy," as well as anxious for others to reach Canada, calling it "Britain's free land, not only free for the white man but for all."[10]

Josiah Henson, born in 1789 in Charles County, Maryland, served as one of the models for Harriet Beecher Stowe's Uncle Tom. His master moved to Kentucky, and there Josiah Henson tried to purchase his freedom. But he was betrayed by his master, who stole his manumission papers, the official documents releasing him from slavery. Henson escaped with his family to Cincinnati and then to Canada. On one occasion, while on the road, he removed his shoes and filled them with water to give his children a drink.[11]

THE LONDON SCHOOL OF PHOTOGRAPHY, 103, NEWGATE STREET. E.C.

Reverend Josiah Henson (seated), born in 1789, escaped from slavery and settled in the Canadian community of Dawn. He made several return trips to Kentucky to help free other slaves. Henson also traveled to Boston and Great Britain to raise money to establish a school for fugitives.

Josiah Henson soon found work as a tenant farmer for a Mr. Hibbard in Dresden near the Canadian border of Lake Erie. With his wages he was able to buy his own pigs, cow, and horse. He later was ordained to the ministry and worked to improve living conditions for the other fugitive slaves. Henson returned several times to Kentucky, once leading away thirty slaves, and later rescuing even more. In all, the number of slaves he helped free totalled 188.[12] He traveled to the country of Great Britain twice before the Civil War to garner support for the antislavery cause and once met Queen Victoria.

In 1842, Reverend Henson and Reverend Hiram Wilson from Massachusetts planned to start a manual-labor school with a grant for fifteen hundred dollars from Quakers in England. The school would teach basic academics, as well as "the practice of some mechanic art" for the boys and "domestic arts" for the girls.[13] They purchased three hundred acres of land for the Institute in the town of Dawn, in Canada West, where they quickly began construction. Fugitives, hearing of the school, were drawn to the area and many established homes on the Institute land.

The land chosen for the Institute was covered with rich forests of black walnut. Reverend Henson conceived of a plan for the settlers to support themselves by selling the valuable lumber. He traveled to Boston to raise money for the construction of a sawmill. The sale of lumber later helped sustain the settlement. In 1851, at

the Great Exhibition in England, the Reverend Henson displayed the black walnut boards that he had planed and polished "in French style, so that they actually shone like a mirror."[14]

Church missions and other associations helped establish settlements where once there had been only wilderness. After the passage of the Fugitive Slave Law in 1850, Henry Bibb, a fugitive and abolitionist lecturer, started a Canadian colony called Refugees' Home. He financed it through contributions as well as through the sale of twenty-five-acre lots. Settlers built small log houses, cleared one to five acres, and raised corn, potatoes, and other vegetables. In 1852, Laura S. Haviland, a Quaker, opened the first school for the settlement. Many drove their oxen teams five or six miles to attend her classes. After six weeks she found her students had learned to read and write.[15] A mission committee of the Presbyterian Church started the Elgin settlement off the shores of Lake Erie. Seventy families entered the settlement during its first year in 1860, purchasing farms of fifty acres at a low cost that could be paid in installments. Within ten years the population had reached one thousand.

A writer named Benjamin Drew toured the cities and settlements of Canada West, interviewing numerous fugitives and recording their words as he went along. These personal accounts were published in a book, *North-Side View of Slavery*, in 1856. Wherever the author went, he encountered fugitives willing to give their testimony, but in

Chatham he realized "more fully than anywhere else . . . the extent of the American exodus." He writes that "at every turn," the traveler "meets members of the African race, single or in groups; he sees them building and painting houses, working in mills, engaged in every handicraft employment."[16]

Before coming to Canada, J. C. Brown had bought his liberty for eighteen hundred dollars. But, as a free man, he was run out of Louisville, Kentucky, for angering some local slaveholders. He ended up bringing his family across the Canadian border to Chatham where he told Benjamin Drew,

> Our children growing up in this country, and not having the fear of any white man, and being taught to read and write, will grow up entirely different from their fathers . . . . Slavery disarms a man of virtue, —of every thing: it prevents his being a man. Anticipation is what we live for, —it makes us anxious to improve ourselves and our children; but the slave anticipates nothing, but the setting of the sun . . . . [17]

Finding Refuge in Great Britain

Although the majority of fugitives who left the United States after the Fugitive Slave Act settled in Canada, many found refuge in Great Britain where antislavery sentiment was strong. What they found was "a less prejudiced society . . . —there were no 'negro pews' in churches, no restrictions on travel, lodgings, or transportation, and no racial slurs on the streets."[18]

For many years British abolitionists had worked with Americans in the antislavery movement. They raised money and lent their support. Americans, such as Frederick Douglass, traveled to Britain to lecture and solicit aid. The money they collected was used to fund schools and newspapers and to purchase the freedom of friends and family. Word of Britain's hospitable climate spread, increasing the number of fugitives. In 1850, William Powell, commenting on his arrival in Britain, wrote, "The change is so sudden . . . that I can hardly believe my senses. I feel for once in my life a man indeed . . . and more the shame for my color-hating country."[19]

Frederick Douglass, sailing to England on a British ship in 1845, was forced to sleep in the stern and was not admitted to the saloon. But once on British soil he discovered he was welcome almost everywhere. Ellen Richardson, a member of the Society of Friends, and others raised one hundred and

Frederick Douglass sailed to England in 1845. The British purchased his freedom and raised the money for him to start the abolitionist newspaper the *North Star*. After the Civil War, Douglass worked to obtain civil rights for women and blacks. While in Washington, he served as an advisor to the presidents, a United States marshal, and a recorder of deeds.

fifty pounds sterling to purchase his liberation. The British also donated twenty-five hundred dollars for Frederick Douglass to establish the *North Star* upon his return.

William and Ellen Craft, upon their arrival in Britain, joined William Wells Brown in travels through England and Scotland. They made many stops along the way, speaking to large audiences on antislavery. William Wells Brown pleaded for their cause and the Crafts told the story of their escape from Georgia—Ellen disguised as a white male slave owner and William as "his" slave. They talked about forced labor, physical abuse, the absence of education, and the separation and destruction of families caused by slavery. The *Liverpool Mercury* reported, "All who see and talk with them cannot but feel a deep thrill of indignation at a system that would rob such persons of their humanity."[20]

In 1851, the Crafts settled at the Ockham School in Surrey, England, where they continued their education. After moving to London a few years later, they supported the free produce movement and also hosted black abolitionists on tours through England. American newspapers published accounts that Ellen Craft missed her family in Georgia and wanted to return to her master. Denying these reports, Ellen wrote in a letter to the editor, published in the British *Anti-Slavery Advocate*:

> The statement is entirely unfounded, for I have never had the slightest inclination whatever of returning to bondage… for I had much rather starve in England, a free woman, than be a slave for the best man that ever breathed upon the American continent.[21]

Many fugitives arrived in England only to find jobs hard to come by and the standard of living relatively poor, yet they never doubted they had made the right choice. Ottobah Cugoana, born in Africa and sold as a slave, escaped to England. From there he wrote:

> Bad as it is, the poorest in England would not change their situation for that of slaves. . . . For the slaves, like animals, are bought and sold, and dealt with as their capricious owners may think fit, even in torturing and tearing them to pieces, and wearing them out with hard labour, hunger and oppression . . . whatever circumstances poor free men may be in, their situation is much superior, beyond any proportion, to that of the hardships and cruelty of modern slavery.[22]

Samuel Ringgold Ward, a fugitive and fervent abolitionist, spent time in both Canada and Great Britain. He had escaped from slavery as an infant, carried north by his mother. He studied classics and theology before becoming an ordained minister. In October 1851, he learned of the arrest of a fugitive slave named Jerry in Syracuse, New York. Ward urged the crowd gathered outside the courthouse during Jerry's trial to liberate him. Several men broke down the door to the courthouse, allowing Jerry to run free. Jerry fled to Canada and Ward soon followed to escape indictment.[23] Ward helped file off Jerry's chains, which were then sent to President Millard Fillmore in a mahogany box.[24]

Ward traveled to Great Britain to speak and was asked by British abolitionists to write the story of his life. *Autobiography of a Fugitive Negro*, published in 1855, tells of Ward's experiences with discrimination. In coming to England, Ward writes that he was in "a land of freedom, of true equality," and yet he realized that he himself had

SOURCE DOCUMENT

An impassioned condemnation of the Fugitive Slave Act passed by Congress in September 1850. The print shows a group of four black men—possibly freedmen—ambushed by a posse of six armed whites in a cornfield. One of the white men fires on them, while two of his companions reload their muskets. Two of the blacks have evidently been hit; one has fallen to the ground while the second staggers, clutching the back of his bleeding head. The two others react with horror.

not changed. He wrote, "I did not feel as some blacks say they felt, upon landing—that I was, for the first time in my life, a man. No, I always felt that; however wronged, maltreated, outraged—still, a man."[25]

Abolishing Slavery

The political climate in the North changed most dramatically with the passage of the Fugitive Slave Law in 1850. Although abolitionists, both black and white, had been actively working to end slavery, others had—to a certain extent— ignored the issue. But the new law pushed the issue to the forefront, forcing the public to take a stand. The capture of fugitives, their return to slavery, and the trials surrounding the more notable fugitive cases caught people's attention, offended their sensibility, and often led to outrage. Bitter debate on slavery, its abolition, and the rights

Thousands of former slaves became soldiers for the North.

of fugitives gave way to extreme polarization between North and South. When Abraham Lincoln won the presidential election in 1860, South Carolinians, unwilling to accept the antislavery candidate, seceded from the Union. Before President Lincoln's inauguration, six more states

withdrew to form the Confederate States of America. After the firing on Fort Sumter in South Carolina on April 12, 1861, four additional states joined the Confederacy. The Civil War had begun.

On January 1, 1863, President Abraham Lincoln issued the Emancipation Proclamation, declaring that all persons held as slaves in the states of rebellion would be "thenceforward and forever free." He also made provisions for the freed slaves to be accepted in the Union Army. Although this proclamation held great symbolic significance, its practical effect remains questionable since it pertained to the states in the Confederacy, but not to border slaveholding states that had remained loyal to the Union. The Confederate states claimed that the federal government should not involve itself in abolishing slavery or protecting the rights of fugitives, but should leave those issues to individual states. Representatives of the free states wished to end slavery, but did not want to lose the support of the border states.

It was not until June 28, 1864, after much debate in Congress, that the Fugitive Slave Act of 1850 was finally repealed. Slavery itself was not officially abolished until the passage of the thirteenth amendment to the Constitution. On January 31, 1865, Congress submitted the amendment to the states for their approval the following article: "Neither slavery nor involuntary servitude, except as a punishment for crime, whereof the party shall have been duly convicted, shall exist within the United States or any

place subject to their jurisdiction." After twenty-seven of the thirty-six states approved the amendment, it was formally adopted on December 18, 1865.

With General Robert E. Lee's surrender to General Ulysses S. Grant at Appomattox Courthouse, Virginia, on April 9, 1865, the Civil War came to an end. Six hundred thousand Americans lay dead as a result of the war when President Lincoln died from an assassin's bullet on April 15, 1865. The nation's wounds were raw, but the Union had been preserved and slavery abolished within it.

The passage of the fifteenth amendment in 1870 guaranteed African Americans the right to vote. In most parts of the country, the Underground Railroad was no longer needed. It had ceased to operate with no great fanfare. But in Cincinnati, Ohio, a formal ceremony marked the occasion. African Americans and whites gathered to hear speeches celebrating both a new beginning and the end of an era, made possible by the passage of the amendment. Noting that "the road was of no further use," Levi Coffin, who had been given the title of "President of the Underground Railroad," recalled that "amid much applause I resigned my office and declared the operation of the Underground Railroad at an end."[26]

During Reconstruction, following the Civil War, former abolitionists and Underground Railroad agents devoted themselves to securing rights, jobs, and education for the newly freed ex-slaves. Yet many of the measures that were passed in Congress were never enforced. In the words of

Frederick Douglass, "they gave freedmen the machinery of liberty, but denied them the steam to put it in motion." In Southern states "the citizenship granted in the fourteenth amendment is practically a mockery, and the right to vote, provided for in the fifteenth amendment, is literally stamped out in face of government."[27]

Yet Frederick Douglass saw reason for hope. Although the freed slaves were "sent away empty-handed, without money, without friends, and without a foot of land to stand upon," they have:

> no reason to despair. . . . The fact that we have endured wrongs and hardships, which would have destroyed any other race; and have increased in numbers and public consideration, ought to strengthen our faith in ourselves and our future. Let us then, wherever we are, whether at the North or at the South, resolutely struggle on in the belief that there is a better day coming, and that we by patience, industry, uprightness, and economy may hasten that better day . . . . Greatness does not come to any people on flowery beds of ease. We must fight to win the prize.[28]

Frederick Douglass called on his people to "resolutely struggle on" just as in previous decades the many fugitives from slavery had done, knowing there was "a better day coming." Their stories are stirring testaments to their love of freedom and the courage it took to find that freedom, and to a system—the Underground Railroad—that brought people from all walks of life together in a common pursuit.

TIMELINE

1619— A Dutch vessel lands in Jamestown, Virginia, bearing the first African slaves to arrive in the British North American colonies.

1688— *April 18*: In Germantown, Pennsylvania, the Mennonites, a Protestant sect, sign an antislavery resolution—the first in North America.

1775— A group of Quakers founds The Pennsylvania Society for Promoting the Abolition of Slavery, the Relief of Negroes Unlawfully Held in Bondage, and for Improving the Condition of the African Race.

1777— Vermont adopts a constitution providing for the emancipation of its slaves.

1783— In a ruling on the case of Quork Walker, a slave who had been denied the freedom he was promised, the Massachusetts Supreme Court abolishes slavery throughout Massachusetts.

1786— *May 12*: A letter from President George Washington marks the first record of Underground Railroad activity.

1789— The Methodist Church formally prohibits members from "buying or selling the bodies or souls of men, women, or children, with an intention to enslave them."

1789— The first known published slave narrative, *The Life of Olaudah Equiano or Gustavus Vassa, the African*, is published in London.

1793— Congress passes the Fugitive Slave Law, giving the slave owner the right to seize a suspected fugitive in any state. This law, however, is generally not enforced.

1793— The Emancipation Act of Upper Canada limits the terms of contracts slaves must serve and prevents the future introduction of slaves into Canada.

1800— *August 30*: A storm foils Gabriel Prosser's plans for a slave insurrection in Richmond, Virginia.

1820— The Missouri Compromise provides for Missouri's admission to the Union as a slave state. Slavery was prohibited in all territory north with the exception of Missouri.

1822— Denmark Vesey plans a slave revolt in Charleston, South Carolina. After the plot is uncovered, thirty-six conspirators are hanged.

1829— David Walker, a free African American, publishes an antislavery pamphlet, "An Appeal to the Colored People of the World," urging slaves to rebel.

1831— *January 1*: William Lloyd Garrison publishes the first issue of *The Liberator*, calling for the universal emancipation of the slave.

1831— A bloody slave revolt led by Nat Turner in Southampton County, Virginia, ends with the capture of the slaves and the hanging of Nat Turner.

1833— Slavery is abolished throughout the British Empire. William Lloyd Garrison meets in Philadelphia with sixty-three delegates from eleven states to form the American Anti-Slavery Society.

1835— Maria W. Stewart, an abolitionist writer, publishes *Productions of Mrs. Maria W. Stewart, presented to the First African Baptist Church and Society,* a series of spiritual meditations on race and abolition.

1837— Women from several state antislavery societies hold the first Anti-Slavery Convention of American Women.

1838— Robert Purvis, an African-American merchant in Philadelphia, organizes the Vigilance Committee, an active branch of the Underground Railroad.

1840— Five hundred delegates attend the World Anti-Slavery Convention in London.

1842— The Reverend Josiah Henson obtains a grant to start a manual-labor school for African-American refugees in Dawn, Canada. William Wells Brown ferries sixty-nine fugitives across Lake Erie from Cleveland to Canada.

1847— Frederick Douglass publishes the first issue of the *North Star,* an abolitionist newspaper, in Rochester, New York.

1848— *April 15*: Seventy-seven slaves board the *Pearl* in an attempt to escape from the city of Washington.

1848— Ex-slave Henry "Box" Brown escapes from Richmond, Virginia, hidden inside a box shipped to Philadelphia. William and Ellen Craft, two slaves from Macon, Georgia, don elaborate disguises and escape by train and boat to Philadelphia.

1849— Harriet Tubman escapes from Dorchester County, Maryland.

1850— The Fugitive Slave Law is enacted, prohibiting anyone from helping a fugitive and allowing for the return of fugitives from one state to another.

1851— *June 5*: The first installment of Harriet Beecher Stowe's *Uncle Tom's Cabin* is published.

1854— Writer and speaker Frances Ellen Watkins Harper gives her first lecture, "Education and the Elevation of the Colored Race."

1854— *May 25*: Fugitive Anthony Burns is arrested in Boston. His trial rocks the nation and kindles antislavery sentiment.

1855— Samuel Ringgold Ward publishes the *Autobiography of a Fugitive Negro*.

1856— Benjamin Drew publishes *North-Side View of Slavery* after visiting Canadian towns settled by fugitives.

1858— Thirty-seven citizens from the towns of Oberlin and Wellington in Ohio are indicted and later freed for rescuing John Price, a fugitive from Kentucky.

1860— The British publish *The Underground Railroad* by the Reverend W. M. Mitchell, a free African American. Revenues are used to help fugitives in Toronto, Canada.

1861— Fugitive Harriet Jacobs publishes her narrative, *Incidents in the Life of a Slave Girl*, under the pseudonym of Linda Brent.

1861— *April 12*: The firing on Fort Sumter marks the beginning of the Civil War.

1863— *January 1*: President Abraham Lincoln issues the Emancipation Proclamation.

1864— *June 28*: The Fugitive Slave Act of 1850 is repealed.

1872— William Still, the son of slaves and an active member of the Pennsylvania Anti-Slavery Society, publishes an eight-hundred-page book, *The Underground Railroad*, which includes detailed records of the lives of fugitives.

1876— *Reminiscences of Levi Coffin*, which tells the story of the Underground Railroad through the eyes of one of its chief operators, is published.

1883— R. C. Smedley publishes *The Underground Railroad in Chester and the Neighboring Counties of Pennsylvania*.

1898— Wilbur Siebert publishes *The Underground Railroad from Slavery to Freedom*, which includes a directory of thirty-two hundred Underground Railroad operators.

CHAPTER NOTES

Chapter 1. The Escape

1. William Wells Brown, *The Travels of William Wells Brown including Narrative of William Wells Brown, A Fugitive Slave and the American Fugitive in Europe*, ed. Paul Jefferson (New York: Markus Wiener Publishing, Inc., 1991), p. 68.

2. Ibid., p. 29.

3. Ibid., p. 38.

4. Ibid., p. 40.

5. Ibid., p. 51.

6. Ibid., p. 63.

Chapter 2. Living in Slavery

1. Stephen Buckley, "U.S., African Blacks Differ on Turning Slave Dungeons into Tourist Attraction," *The Washington Post*, April 17, 1995, p. A10.

2. Herbert S. Klein, *The Middle Passage* (Princeton, N.J.: Princeton University Press, 1978), p. 229.

3. Daniel P. Mannix, *Black Cargoes: A History of the Atlantic Slave Trade* (New York: Viking Press, 1962), p. 105.

4. Ibid., pp. 113–115.

5. Gustavus Vassa, *The Life of Olaudah Equiano or Gustavus Vassa, the African (1789)*, reprinted in *Great Slave Narratives*, ed. Arna Bontemps (Boston: Beacon Press, 1969), p. 28.

6. Klein, p. 123.

7. Kenneth Stampp, *The Peculiar Institution* (New York: Knopf, 1956), p. 24.

8. Harriet Beecher Stowe, *A Key to Uncle Tom's Cabin; Presenting the Original Facts and Documents upon Which the Story is Founded. Together with Corroborative Statements Verifying the Truth of the Work* (Boston: John P. Jewett and Co., 1853), p. 11.

9. Benjamin Drew, *A North-Side View of Slavery: The Refugee or the Narratives of Fugitive Slaves in Canada Related by Themselves* (Boston: John P. Jewett and Co., 1856), p. 122.

10. Stowe, p. 10.

11. Kenneth M. Stampp, "Chattels Personal," *Slavery in American Society*, eds. Richard D. Brown and Stephen G. Rabe (Lexington, Mass.: D.C. Heath & Co., 1976), p. 94.

12. Pencil copy, Lewis Papers, interviewed by Emmy Wilson and Claude W. Anderson, date unknown, from *Weevils in the Wheat: Interviews with Virginia Ex-Slaves*, eds. Charles L. Perdue, Jr., Thomas E. Barden, and Robert K. Phillips (Charlottesville, Va.: University Press of Virginia, 1976), p. 100.

13. William Still, *The Underground Railroad* (Philadelphia: Anti-Slavery Society, 1872; reprinted by Johnson Publishing Company, Chicago, 1970), p. 143.

14. Drew, p. 275.

15. Ibid., p. 41.

16. Ibid., p. 184.

17. Stampp, *Slavery in American Society*, pp. 94–105.

18. Marion Starling, *The Slave Narrative: Its Place in American History* (Washington, D.C.: Howard University Press, 1988), p. 118.

19. Drew, p. 178.

20. "Narrative of Margaret Ward and Infant Son, Samuel Ringgold Ward," in Charles L. Blockson, *The Underground Railroad* (New York: Prentice Hall Press, 1987), p. 101.

21. Statistics taken from the U.S. Bureau of the Census, quoted in Stampp, *The Peculiar Institution,* pp. 30–31, and Ira Berlin, *Slaves Without Masters: The Free Negro in the Antebellum South* (New York: The New Press, 1974), pp. 396–399.

22. Leon F. Litwack, "Slavery to Freedom," *Slavery in American Society,* pp. 82–86.

23. Eric Foner, "The Republicans and Race," *Slavery in American Society,* p. 210.

24. "Quaker Resolution against Slavery, 1652," in *Black Protest: History, Documents, and Analyses: 1619 to the Present*, ed. Joanne Grant (New York: Fawcett Publications, 1968), p. 26.

25. Wilbur H. Siebert, *The Underground Railroad from Slavery to Freedom* (New York: Macmillan Company, 1898), p. 94.

26. Ibid.

27. Ibid., p. 96.

28. David Walker, *Appeal* in *Black Protest,* p. 85.

29. Ibid., p. 69.

30. Benjamin Quarles, *Black Abolitionists* (New York: Oxford University Press, 1969), pp. 29–30.

31. Charles H. Nichols, *Many Thousand Gone: The Ex-Slaves' Account of Their Bondage and Freedom* (Bloomington, Ind.: Indiana University Press, 1963), p. 132.

32. Betty Fladeland, *Men and Brothers: Anglo-American Antislavery Cooperation* (Urbana, Ill.: University of Illinois Press, 1972), p. 269.

33. Frederic S. Voss, *Majestic in his Wrath: A Pictorial Life of Frederick Douglass* (Washington, D.C.: Smithsonian Institution Press, 1995), p. v.

34. *Black Protest,* p. 84.

35. Siebert, p. 323.

Chapter 3. The Flight

1. Wilbur H. Siebert, *The Underground Railroad from Slavery to Freedom* (New York: Macmillan Company, 1898), p. 33.

2. Ibid., p. 45.

3. Jane Pyatt to Thelma Dunston (interviewer), January 15, 1937, Virginia State Library, in *Weevils in the Wheat: Interviews with Virginia Ex-Slaves*, eds. Charles L. Perdue, Jr., Thomas E. Barden, and Robert K. Phillips (Charlottesville, Va.: University Press of Virginia, 1976), p. 234.

4. Siebert, p. 54; and Benjamin Drew, *A North-Side View of Slavery: The Refugee or the Narratives of Fugitive Slaves in Canada Related by Themselves* (Boston: John P. Jewett and Co., 1856), p. 283.

5. Drew, pp. 18–64.

6. Siebert, p. 57.

7. Letter from Isaac Forman to William Still (February 20, 1854), in William Still, *The Underground Railroad* (Philadelphia: Anti-Slavery Society, 1872, reprinted Chicago: Johnson Publishing Company, 1970), p. 50.

8. Siebert, p. 37.

9. Ibid., p. 87.

10. Ibid., p. 89.

11. Ibid., p. 147.

12. Ibid., p. 33.

13. Letter from Frederick Douglass to Wilbur Siebert (March 27, 1893), in Siebert, p. 126.

14. Reverend C. W. B. Gordon, date unknown, interviewer Susie R. C. Byrd, in *Weevils in the Wheat*, p. 110.

15. Marjory Stoneman Douglas, *The Everglades: River of Grass* (Sarasota, Fla.: Pineapple Press, 1947), pp. 185–245.

Chapter 4. The Fugitives

1. Charles L. Blockson, *Hippocrene Guide to the Underground Railroad* (New York: Hippocrene Books, 1994), p. 12.

2. *Weevils in the Wheat: Interviews with Virginia Ex-Slaves*, eds. Charles L. Perdue, Jr., Thomas E. Barden, and Robert K. Phillips (Charlottesville, Va.: University Press of Virginia, 1976), p. 85.

3. *Frederick Douglass, Narrative of the Life of Frederick Douglass, an American Slave* (Boston: Anti-Slavery Office, 1845), reprinted in *The Classic Slave Narratives*, ed. Henry Louis Gates, Jr. (New York: Penguin Books, 1987), pp. 256–277.

4. William Still, *The Underground Railroad* (Philadelphia: Anti-Slavery Society, 1872, reprinted Chicago: Johnson Publishing Company, 1970), p. 112.

5. Ibid., pp. 67–73.

6. Henry Louis Gates, Jr., ed., *Classic Slave Narratives* (New York: Penguin Books, 1987), p. xvii.

7. Linda Brent, *Incidents in the Life of a Slave Girl* (Boston: original publisher unknown, 1861), reprinted in *Classic Slave Narratives*, p. 437.

8. William Craft, *Running a Thousand Miles for Freedom; or, The Escape of William and Ellen Craft from Slavery* (London: W. Tweedie, 1860), reprinted in *Great Slave Narratives* ed. Arna Bontemps (Boston: Beacon Press, 1969), p. 271.

9. Ibid., p. 289.

10. Ibid., p. 310.

11. Ibid., p. 312.

12. Ibid., p. 316.

13. Ibid., p. 315.

14. Letter from William Wells Brown to Frederick Douglass (September 10, 1851), reprinted in C. Peter Ripley, ed., *Black Abolitionist Papers, Vol. I: The British Isles 1830-65*, Document 44 (Chapel Hill, N.C.: The University of North Carolina Press, 1986), pp. 302–305.

Chapter 5. Famous Conductors

1. *Weevils in the Wheat: Interviews with Virginia Ex-Slaves*, eds. Charles L. Perdue, Jr., Thomas E. Barden, and Robert K. Phillips (Charlottesville, Va.: University Press of Virginia, 1976), p. 85.

2. Wilbur H. Siebert, *The Underground Railroad from Slavery to Freedom* (New York: Macmillan Company, 1898), p. 189.

3. Ibid., p. 187.

4. Ibid., p. 188.

5. Benjamin Quarles, *Black Abolitionists* (New York: Oxford University Press, 1969), p. 146.

6. Louis Filler, *The Crusade Against Slavery* (Algonac, Mich.: Reference Publications, 1986), pp. 201–202.

7. Filler, p. 203; Quarles, p. 164; and Siebert, pp. 157–160.

8. Filler, p. 201.

9. Siebert, p. 110.

10. R.C. Smedley, *History of the Underground Railroad in Chester and the Neighboring Counties of Pennsylvania* (Lancaster, Pa.: Office of the Journal, 1883, reprinted New York: Negro Universities Press, 1968), p. 354.

11. Ibid., pp. 355–356.

12. Julie Winch, "Harriet Forten Purvis," *Notable Black American Women* (Detroit: Gale Research, 1992), p. 901.

13. William Still, *The Underground Railroad* (Philadelphia: Anti-Slavery Society, 1872, reprinted Chicago: Johnson Publishing Company, 1970), p. 737.

14. Siebert, p. 346.

15. Levi Coffin, *Reminiscences of Levi Coffin* (Cincinnati: Robert Clarke & Co., 1876), pp. 108–109.

16. Ibid., pp. 111–112.

17. Ibid., p. 323.

18. Ibid., pp. 268–269.

19. Ibid., p. 299.

20. Ibid., p. 301.

21. Maria W. Stewart, *Productions of Mrs. Maria W. Stewart, presented to the First African Baptist Church and Society* (Boston: Friends of Freedom and Virtue, 1835), reprinted in *Spiritual Narratives*, with an introduction by Sue E. Houchins (New York: Oxford University Press, 1988), p. 5.

22. Ibid., p. 17.

23. Still, p. 790.

Chapter 6. On Trial

1. John Paynter, *Fugitives of the Pearl* (Washington, D.C.: Associated Publishers, 1930).

2. Daniel Drayton, *Personal Memoir of Daniel Drayton, for Four Years and Four Months a Prisoner (for Charity's Sake) in Washington Jail, including a Narrative of the Voyage and Capture of the Schooner Pearl* (Boston: Bela Marsh, 1855), p. 85.

3. Ibid., p. 119.

4. *Trial of Anthony Burns (written by an anonymous observer)* (Boston: Fetridge and Company, 1854), reprinted with a new foreword by Donald Franklin Joyce (Northbrook, Ill.: Metro Books, 1972), p. 8.

5. Ibid., pp. 9–10.

6. Ibid., p. 9; and Marion Gleason McDougall, *Fugitive Slaves, 1619–1865* (Cambridge, Mass.: Harvard University Press, 1891), p. 145.

7. McDougall, p. 46.

8. *Trial of Anthony Burns*, p. 85.

9. Charles H. Nichols, *Many Thousand Gone: The Ex-Slaves' Account of Their Bondage and Freedom* (Bloomington, Ind.: Indiana University Press, 1963), p. 156.

10. McDougall, p. 46.

11. Wilbur H. Siebert, *The Underground Railroad from Slavery to Freedom* (New York: Macmillan Company, 1898), pp. 336–337; and McDougall, pp. 49–50.

Chapter 7. The Promised Land

1. Levi Coffin, *Reminiscences of Levi Coffin* (Cincinnati: Robert Clarke & Co., 1876), p. 253.

2. Wilbur H. Siebert, *The Underground Railroad from Slavery to Freedom* (New York: Macmillan Company, 1898), p. 221.

3. Marion Starling, *The Slave Narrative: Its Place in American History* (Washington, D.C.: Howard University Press, 1988), p. 39.

4. Siebert, pp. 221–222.

5. Ibid., pp. 203–232.

6. Ibid., p. 253.

7. *Weevils in the Wheat: Interviews with Virginia Ex-Slaves*, eds. Charles L. Perdue, Jr., Thomas E. Barden, and Robert K. Phillips (Charlottesville, Va.: University Press of Virginia, 1976), pp. 156–157.

8. William Still, *The Underground Railroad* (Philadelphia: Anti-Slavery Society, 1872, reprinted Chicago: Johnson Publishing Company, 1970), p. 191.

9. Ibid., pp. 192–195.

10. Ibid., p. 199.

11. Josiah Henson, *Father Henson's Story of His Own Life* (Boston: John. P. Jewett and Co., 1858), p. 112.

12. Charles H. Nichols, *Many Thousand Gone: The Ex-Slaves' Account of Their Bondage and Freedom* (Bloomington, Ind.: Indiana University Press, 1963), p. 161.

13. Henson, p. 169.

14. Ibid., p. 188.

15. Laura S. Haviland, *A Woman's Life-Work* (Chicago: Publishing Association of Friends, 1881), p. 193.

16. Benjamin Drew, *A North-Side View of Slavery: The Refugee or the Narratives of Fugitive Slaves in Canada Related by Themselves* (Boston: John P. Jewett and Co., 1856), p. 234.

17. Ibid., p. 248.

18. C. Peter Ripley, ed., *Black Abolitionist Papers Vol. I: The British Isles 1830-65*, Document 44 (Chapel Hill, N.C.: The University of North Carolina Press, 1986), Introduction, p. 33.

19. Letter from William P. Powell to Sydney Howard Gay, December 12, 1850, in Ripley, p. 33.

20. Benjamin Quarles, *Black Abolitionists* (New York: Oxford University Press, 1969), p. 137.

21. Charles H. Nichols, *Many Thousand Gone: The Ex-Slaves' Account of their Bondage and Freedom* (Bloomington, Ind.: Indiana University Press, 1963), p. 152.

22. William Naish, *The Negro's Friend Consisting of Anecdotes of the African Race,* 2nd edition, (London: 183?), p. 16.

23. Samuel Ringgold Ward, *Autobiography of a Fugitive Negro* (London: John Snow, 1855, reprinted New York: Arno Press, 1968), pp. 117–118.

24. Nichols, p. 159.

25. Ward, p. 236.

26. Coffin, p. 712.

27. Frederick Douglass, extract from a speech given August 1, 1880, Elmira, New York, included in Frederick Douglass, *Life and Times of Frederick Douglass* (Hartford: Park Publishing Company, 1881, reprinted by Citadel Press, Secaucus, N.J., 1983), pp. 511–512.

28. Ibid., pp. 514–515.

FURTHER READING

Bordewich, Fergus M. *Bound for Canaan: The Epic Story of the Underground Railroad, America's First Civil Rights Movement.* New York: HarperCollins Publishers, Inc., 2005.

Still, William. *The Underground Railroad: A Record of Facts, Authentic Narratives, Letters & c., Narrating the Hardships, Hair-Breadth Escapes and Death Struggles of...& Others or Witnessed by the Author.* New York: Benediction Books, 2009.

Tobin, Jacqueline. *From Midnight to Dawn: The Last Tracks of the Underground Railroad.* New York: Random House, Inc., 2007.

Burgan, Michael. *The Underground Railroad.* New York: Chelsea House, 2006.

Landau, Elaine. *Fleeing to Freedom on the Underground Railroad: The Courageous Slaves, Agents, and Conductors.* Minneapolis: Twenty-First Century Books, 2006.

Lantier, Patricia. *Harriet Tubman: Conductor on the Underground Railroad.* New York: Crabtree, 2010.

INTERNET ADDRESSES

National Geographic Online Presents: The Underground Railroad
<http://www.nationalgeographic.com/railroad/>
> *A great way to explore and research the Underground Railroad through the National Geographic perspective and insights.*

National Underground Railroad Freedom Center
<http://www.freedomcenter.org/underground-railroad/>
> *This unique web site offers a vast array of knowledge on both the Underground Railroad and slavery.*

The Underground Railroad: Escape from Slavery
<http://www2.scholastic.com/browse/search?query=underground+railroad>
> *Find out what it was like to escape to freedom on the Underground Railroad in these interactive activities.*

INDEX